Basic Behavior Modification

New Vistas in Counseling Series
Series Editors—Garry Walz and Libby Benjamin
In collaboration with **ERIC** *Counseling and Personnel Services Information Center*

Structured Groups for Facilitating Development: Acquiring Life Skills, Resolving Life Themes, and Making Life Transitions, Volume 1
Knott, J. E., Ph.D. and Drum, D. J., Ph.D.

New Methods for Delivering Human Services, Volume 2
Jones, G. B., Ph.D., Dayton, C., Ph.D. and Gelatt, H. B., Ph.D.

Systems Change Strategies in Educational Settings, Volume 3
Arends, R. I., Ph.D. and Arends, J. H., Ph.D.

Counseling Older Persons: Careers, Retirement, Dying, Volume 4
Sinick, D., Ph.D.

Parent Education and Elementary Counseling, Volume 5
Lamb, J. and Lamb, W., Ph.D.

Counseling in Correctional Environments, Volume 6
Bennett, L. A., Ph.D., Rosenbaum, T. S., Ph.D. and McCullough, W. R., Ph.D.

Transcultural Counseling: Needs, Programs and Techniques, Volume 7
Walz, J., Ph.D., Benjamin, L., Ph.D., et al.

Career Resource Centers, Volume 8
Meerbach, J., Ed.D.

Behavior Modification Handbook for Helping Professionals, Volume 9
Mehrabian, A., Ph.D.

Basic Behavior Modification

Albert Mehrabian, Ph.D.

University of California, Los Angeles

*Vol. 9 in the New Vistas in Counseling
Series, in collaboration with ERIC Counseling
and Personnel Services Information Center
Series Editors*—Garry R. Walz and Libby Benjamin

HUMAN SCIENCES PRESS
72 Fifth Avenue   3 Henrietta Street
NEW YORK, NY 10011 ● LONDON, WC2E 8LU

Library of Congress Catalog Number 77-85582
ISBN: 0-87705-322-7

Copyright © 1978 Human Sciences Press
72 Fifth Avenue, New York, N.Y. 10011

Copyright is claimed until 1983. Thereafter, all portions of the work covered by this copyright will be in the public domain. This work was developed under a contract with the National Institute of Education, Department of Health, Education, and Welfare. However, the content does not necessarily reflect the position or policy of that agency, and no United States Government endorsement of these materials should be inferred.

Albert Mehrabian, Tactics of Social Influence, © 1970. By permission of Prentice-Hall, Inc. Englewood Cliffs, N.J.

Printed in the United States of America
89 987654321

Library of Congress Cataloging in Publication Data

Mehrabian, Albert.
    Basic behavior modification.

    (New vistas in counseling series; v. 9)
    Includes bibliographical references.
    1. Behavior modification. I. Title. II. Series.
BF637.B4M39   153.8'5   77-85582
ISBN 0-87705-322-7

TABLE OF CONTENTS

44899

FOREWORD

E. Robert Jones has said, "It is easier to act yourself into a new way of thinking than to think yourself into a new way of acting." This statement very succinctly expresses the underlying principle of behavior modification, the theory that if behaviors can be changed and successfully maintained over time, then attitudes and feelings will also change to become consistent with the new behaviors. Such an approach to counseling contains profound implications not only for the role of the counselor but also for the quality or kind of relationship that develops between counselor and client. Rather than serving as an empathic, accepting, clarifying sounding board, the counselor who utilizes behavioral techniques assumes a teaching stance and guides the client through structured learning situations.

The idea of planning changes in another's behavior, of keeping track of another's progress, of deliberately shaping another's actions may seem dehumanizing to many of us initially. And surely such techniques will not fit all situations. When a behavioral approach has the potential to bring about improvement, however, it behooves all counselors to understand the theory behind it, to become familiar with the basic techniques, and to have the skills to practice it effectively. Knowing that few counselors have been trained in behavior modification and believing that the truly qualified counselor should possess a repertoire of helping skills, we asked Dr. Albert Mehrabian to prepare a manuscript for us that would outline the basic principles of behavior modification, define and describe how behaviors are learned and/or changed, and provide information about a number of methods which counselors could immediately adopt and use in their own work settings.

Using dozens of everyday, common examples that all of us will recognize from our own experience, ranging from the child who won't pick up his/her toys to complex marital conflict, the author removes the mystique from behavior modification. He explains behavioral terminology clearly, concisely, in words we can all understand, and suggests techniques that can be used even by psychologically untrained persons.

The truth of the matter is that you all engage in behavior modification every day, self- as well as other-directed, although you may be unaware of it. You practice modeling, negative and positive reinforcement, shaping, stimulus control, or a token economy almost unconsciously and without thought. Reading this manuscript will help you identify and put a name to some of the things you do daily. This increased understanding can then help you become more purposeful in what you do and thus more effective in reaching your planned-for outcomes.

The author provides a list of resources into which interested readers may delve for information beyond that presented in the monograph. Another rich storehouse of resources is the ERIC collection, and we hope you will explore it as well for the latest in ongoing behavioral programs and practices. We guarantee that your search of the ERIC system will be rewarding and that you will be positively reinforced to continue learning about and becoming skillful in this provocative field.

Garry R. Walz and Libby Benjamin

This chapter contains an overview of the basic principles of behavior modification and presents a method of defining problems so that they can be approached with behavior modification techniques.

Chapter 1

DEFINING THE PROBLEM

There is a kind of inertia in people's behavior that makes change difficult and distressing. It is easier to act the way we always have than it is to change our behavior, even though that behavior may be unsatisfactory and even troublesome.

People's ability to change their own behavior and to influence that of others is one of their most important tools for adapting to life situations; it comes into play in their private lives, in their home, social, vocational, and political environments, and it has a tremendous effect on human relations. If people are unwilling or unable to realize their potential for change and influence, they are likely to experience frustration in their personal relationships.

Unwillingness or inability to change is due in part to the fact that when we *do* arrive at a common-sense or intuitive solution to a problem, it often ends in failure. So we find ourselves reverting to our old ways. In other words, this failure to find workable solutions can cause inertia. But why do we fail?

A major obstacle to changing behavior is the lack of guiding principles that are simple enough to be applied successfully in everyday problem situations. We lack such rules partly because we are somehow repulsed by the idea that our own behavior—or anybody elses's—might be explained and compartmentalized by impersonal rules. Most of us have trouble discussing our methods for dealing with others; we may *feel* that a particular reaction will help solve a problem but be unable to describe any principle that led us to that conclusion. We tend to be skeptical of the suggestion that many behaviors could be predicted reasonably well or changed in terms of some set of rules. Our humanistic values have discouraged us from approaching the workings of our own lives and personal relationships as we approach inanimate objects. While we have established numerous principles for dealing with the technical aspects of our environment, we shy away from "rules" for coping with the more complex and mysterious realm of human interaction.

On the basis of such recent developments, our present effort is designed to counteract (1) the widespread feeling that people's behaviors can't be categorized or made subject to "rules," and (2) the tendency to consider interpersonal problems to be too complex and confusing for the layman to deal with.

This monograph deals, then, with behavior modification. We cite some principles and then illustrate their application to several classes of situations where change occurs or is desired. Our examples, for the most part, have been drawn from the common situations that we all might encounter at some times in our lives.

Problem situations seem to dominate our discussions since they illustrate most dramatically the need for change and the characteristic aspects of the processes involved. But our approach isn't entirely problem oriented—most of the principles discussed can also serve to "make a good situation better."

We discuss many interrelated techniques that are drawn from learning theory and research and are known generally as *behavior modification* (Bachrach, 1962; Bandura, 1969; Eysenck, 1960; Lundin, 1969; Mehrabian, 1970; Mischel, 1968; Ullmann & Krasner, 1969; Wolpe, 1969). Thus the approach that has been used throughout involves just a few basic concepts and the relationships among them.

How Behavior Modification Is Different

The behavior modification approach differs in several aspects from the more familiar Freudian (Erikson, 1963; Freud, 1935; Rapaport, 1959) and other related psychodynamic psychologies (Rogers, 1951). One distinction is that it focuses on specific behaviors rather than unobservable internal processes and conflicts. It therefore includes procedures for attempting change that can be readily measured and assessed as to their effectiveness, whereas changes in internal conflict are more difficult to measure. But, more important, behavior modification differs from psychodynamic approaches in that it involves very few concepts that need to be understood and remembered before they can be applied. Readers are thus provided with (1) a broad set of guidelines for identifying recurrent patterns in their own or others' behavior, and (2) a set of rules and procedures for changing such behavior, which should help them avoid the intuitive trial-and-error methods for problem solving that are frequently time consuming and, worse, ineffective.

Defining the Behavioral Problem

The first step in the attempt to influence behavior is, very simply, to define the problem. If "define the problem" sounds superfluous—an unnecessarily obvious beginning —you may find it interesting to observe for a time just how vague most people are when it comes to pinpointing their difficulties. A precise definition of one's problem is important because it provides a goal, a focus for one's efforts, which in itself helps to alleviate frustration.

If we can find a way to expand the statement of a problem to a concrete list of the specific behaviors that constitute it, one major obstacle to the solution of the problem will have been overcome. In other words, the initial ambiguity with which most people analyze their interpersonal problems tends to contribute to their feeling of helplessness in coping with them. Knowing which specific behaviors are involved, and thereby what changes in those behaviors will solve the problem, provides a definite goal for action—and having that goal can lend a great sense of relief.

Let's begin this business of definition by examining two situations in which behavioral changes are desirable.

Rachel: My husband is sometimes so rational, so unemotional, that he seems cold and cruel. This sort of attitude doesn't seem intentional, nor is it lasting, but when it does happen there is nothing I can do but hopelessly accept it while it lasts.

Reuben: I have two roommates and generally we get along pretty well, but one of them often wants to have things his own way and this becomes a problem in what would otherwise be trivial situations. For example, if I am cooking, he will be there with detailed instructions on how I should go about it. He decides, or tries to decide, when the apartment will be cleaned and who will do just what job. In a host of other circumstances, he often tries to impose his will on my other roommate and me, and the decisions he makes often seem arbitrary, without any particular reason or logic. Since he is our roommate and a good friend in many ways, we have been hesitant to approach him about this situation for fear of creating an atmosphere in which none of us could live comfortably. Certainly we will have to approach him someday, but since his tendency to issue menial instructions amounts almost to a passion, we do not see how it will do much good.

There is a marked difference in these descriptions. From Reuben's statement it is easy to see which of the troublesome roommate's behaviors are a source of irritation and discomfort to the other two. For example, he told them how to cook and when to clean. If Reuben had said merely, "I have a roommate who really irritates us by being so overbearing and frequently imposing his will on others," the statement would have lacked enough detail to be helpful. As it was, his statement indicated more clearly how to proceed in changing the irritating behaviors. It was desirable, for instance, to discourage the roommate's unsolicited advice and to minimize the frequency with which he ordered the others to carry out household chores.

In contrast, Rachel said she sometimes found her husband unemotional and unresponsive, but did not specify the behaviors that were upsetting to her. If she had gone no further, it would have been difficult to proceed to a meaningful solution. She had to describe exactly what she meant when she called his behavior "unemotional." When she was encouraged to give very detailed illustrations, certain recurrent behavior patterns became apparent. For example, when she told her husband about a problem she was having with their child, she was hoping he would offer some assistance or moral support, such as, "We could take the baby along with us tonight." Instead, he often responded with an intellectual observation about child rearing. To Rachel, a more sympathetic response from him would have indicated more willingness on his part to help her out, to spend time with—and do more for—their baby. Again, the critical point was for her to elaborate specific examples and describe in each case exactly what she said and did and what he did in response. With these specifics, she was in a better position to focus on the behaviors that needed change. The first step in the definition process, then, is to obtain an expression of the problem in terms of specific components rather than in vague generalities. (As already mentioned, it's surprising to note how many of us *do* stop at generalities.) After eliciting one detailed illustration, we request a second one, and then a third, and so forth, until perhaps half a dozen illustrations are obtained. Provided with such a set, we can then begin to see certain patterns, certain characteristic qualities in the behavior of the participants and in the qualities of the setting, all of which form the basis for understanding the difficulty. It is essential to draw out as many details as possible. More specifically, the common patterns to look for among the examples are (1) the undesirable behaviors that are associated with distress and that seem to be beyond the control of the persons involved, and (2) the implied direction of change, that is, the implied desirable behaviors that would relieve the distress and frustration.

Ranking the Problem Behaviors

Once we have established the specific behaviors that need to be changed (increased or decreased) in a given situation, we can further clarify the nature of the problem by deciding just how severe each problem behavior is relative to the others—the second step in defining a problem. For example, if we conclude that a problem situation involves seven undesirable behaviors, those behaviors are ordered from one (most distressing) to seven (least distressing). With such an ordered list, we can go even further and estimate the needed increases and decreases in the "frequency" of each behavior. That is, we can estimate the number of times a behavior *actually* occurs, as well as how often we *want* it to occur during a given period of time.

There are several reasons for ranking the troublesome behaviors in this way. First of all, experiments have shown that the least severe problem behavior is the easiest to change successfully. And success encourages perseverance —people are much more likely to continue to a more challenging difficulty if they've been able to "conquer" the first ones they faced. Also, the successful change of some less severe problem behaviors can frequently provide people with necessary coping skills—a kind of "on-the-job training"—so that they are better equipped to deal with the more difficult stages of the problem when they finally approach them. So, establishing an ordered list and attacking the problem in that order increases the possibility of success at each stage and the likelihood that a person will see a problem through to its finish.

What else contributes to the severity of the problem besides its distressing quality? One thing is the *frequency* with which it occurs and its "uncontrollability." While either a high frequency or an uncontrollable quality in a problem behavior can indicate severity, a combination of both points to pronounced severity.

SUMMARY

This chapter discussed behavior modification as distinct from Freudian and similar psychologies in that the former deals with specific, observable behaviors instead of a complex network of unobservable internal processes. The first step in behavior modification, defining the problem behavior, was also identified and discussed.

This chapter begins with the details of instrumental learning which led to the *shaping* technique in behavior modification. Our analysis shows how maladaptive behaviors are inadvertently taught or learned and further discussion provides information about a number of methods which can be used to speed up behavior change.

Chapter 2

REWARDING "GOOD MISTAKES"

REWARD, PUNISHMENT, AND BEHAVIOR CHANGE

You have carefully defined the problem. Now comes the hard part: How do you go about bridging the gap between what your problem situation is *now* and what you would ultimately like it to be? Some answers may be found in the principles of learning. These principles are based on experiments that explored the conditions under which an individual replaces old behaviors with new ones, or simply acquires new ones. They are, therefore, most relevant to our consideration of behavior modification and social influence.

The area of learning contributes a major concept for explaining change—*reinforcement.* There are two categories of reinforcement, positive and negative. Broadly speaking, positive reinforcement means rewarding people for exhibiting a specific behavior. Those experiences or things that are intrinsically satisfying, such as the gratification of basic physical needs (hunger, sex), are obvious positive reinforcers. There are other weaker reinforcers—doing something for another that they like, for example, or giving them an opportunity to do something they enjoy. When a man buys his wife her favorite flowers or takes his son to the movies, he is behaving in a positively reinforcing way. Although he may not actually be thinking about reinforcing some specific behavior of his wife or child, he nevertheless is effecting change in some behavior of each one.

Negative reinforcement is punishment for exhibiting a certain behavior, and it ranges from painful physical stimulation and deprivation to weaker reinforcers such as verbal criticism, hostility, or simple expressions of dislike.[1]

Experiments have shown a consistent relationship between reinforcement of behavior and the subsequent frequency with which that behavior occurs (Ferster & Skinner, 1957). The shorter the delay in positively reinforcing a behavior after it occurs, the greater the *increase* in the frequency of that behavior. Similarly, the shorter the delay in delivering a negative reinforcement, the greater the *drop* in the frequency of behavior (Azrin & Holz, 1966). Some very precise information has been obtained about how closely in time reinforcement must follow a behavior in order to be effective (Ferster & Skinner, 1957; Skinner, 1961). For our purposes, we need only note that, in general, the sooner a reinforcement can follow an act, the greater its effect.

As we stated above, a behavior tends to be repeated more frequently after it is positively reinforced and less frequently after it is negatively reinforced. In other words, there is experimental justification for our common-sense

[1]See Appendix A of Mehrabian & Ksionzky, 1974, for the theoretical and experimental justification of the preceding somewhat unconventional definitions of positive and negative reinforcements.

assumption that people who are rewarded for something they do will be more likely to do that thing again, and that they are less likely to repeat behaviors for which they have been punished.

In choosing reinforcers, we must consider an individual's likes and dislikes. To a child who loves Walt Disney movies, going to see "Bambi" can be rewarding and, if one chooses, reinforcing. If the child likes candy, receiving a chocolate bar can be reinforcing; if the child likes baseball, being taken to a World Series game could be a positive reinforcer. To an adult, sincere compliments about his or her character or looks can be reinforcing. Success at work can be reinforcing, as can an increase in pay or a bonus. In short, effective reinforcers are simply the things any given person would like to have or be able to do. Will the same things be reinforcing to everyone? No more so than the same things are equally desirable to everyone.

If there are two desirable rewards that can be given, the more reinforcing one can be determined simply by allowing the person a choice and observing which one he or she chooses or, given more time, which one he or she chooses to carry out first or more often (Premack, 1965). In other words, rewards can be ordered in terms of their reinforcing strength by asking the person to order his or her preferences. In this way we might discover, for instance, that a child would most prefer to go to the movies, next to play in the park, finally to have some candy.

Sometimes we may have only vague ideas about what kinds of rewards will be desirable to an individual. In such cases simple questioning often provides some answers. One could obviously ask a child, "What would you like to do?" or, "What are your most favorite things?" Adults can be asked similar questions, or they can be asked for a list of favorite things. Once people tell of their preferences, we can order the preferences in terms of their importance to them and thereby derive a list of possible reinforcers.

It is extremely important to select reinforcers whose effectiveness does not diminish with repeated use, because in order to influence behavior the reinforcer needs to be used repeatedly. Food, for one, is a reinforcer whose effectiveness diminishes rapidly. When a child is reinforced with a candy bar for the tenth time, the child's preference for it, relative to other things that he or she might find reinforcing, drops drastically, and the candy thus ceases to be a very effective reinforcer. In contrast, the repeated use of very small amounts of candy as a reward might not detract substantially from its reinforcing quality.

The entire class of so-called "social reinforcers" (expressions of liking, appreciation, and encouragement, which may be communicated either verbally or nonverbally) also has a tendency to deteriorate with frequent use, particularly with adults. So if we followed every occurrence of someone's desirable behavior with a smile or pleasant comment, it's likely that the person would cease to appreciate our tactics before long—as with too much of any good thing, it would be taken for granted. Of course, one way to avoid this problem of diminishing effectiveness in any situation is to vary the reinforcers used.

Another thing to keep in mind in using reinforcers is to select, among several similar ones, those over which one has the most control. So, in a home where it would be unrealistic to keep food under lock and key, food would not be an effective reinforcer because it is already relatively accessible to a child. But in a school setting where food is not generally available to children, it can be used more effectively as a reinforcer.

Schedules of Reinforcement

The effectiveness of reinforcement, that is, the lasting value of the change induced by it, may also vary according to the schedules of reinforcement used (Ferster & Skinner, 1957).

Suppose it is desirable to increase the frequency of a behavior and that an effective reward has been found for the person who produces that behavior. It would then be necessary to decide *how often* to reward the behavior to best obtain the desired result.

In psychological terminology, *continuous reinforcement* means to reinforce a behavior every time it occurs. When a wife responds with warmth and affection every time her husband brings her flowers, she is reinforcing his flower-buying behavior on a continuous schedule. *Partial reinforcement* generally means to reinforce a behavior only after particular occurrences (Morse, 1966). A special instance of partial reinforcement is *fixed ratio reinforcement,* in which the ratio of nonreinforced to reinforced occurrences is constant—the behavior is reinforced after a fixed number of times it occurs, say every third time. In real-life situations, fixed ratio reinforcement could be illustrated by an elevator salesperson who receives a commission after each four elevators he or she sells. Every fourth occurrence of selling an elevator is reinforced on a fixed ratio schedule. With this schedule, it is typically found that immediately after reinforcement there is a brief pause before the person being reinforced resumes activity at the same rate as before reinforcement. In other words, our elevator salesperson would probably take it easy for a day or so following the bonus payment before wholeheartedly resuming work.

A more interesting and frequently seen version is *variable ratio reinforcement,* in which the ratio of reinforced to nonreinforced occurrences varies—sometimes a behavior might be rewarded after five occurrences, at other times after two. Consider, for instance, the results of spiking the ball when playing volleyball. If the ball lands as intended, leaving the opponent unable to return it, then the spike would provide positive reinforcement. But if the ball lands in the net or outside the court, it would be a nonreinforced or negatively reinforced behavior. For moderately good players, chances are that they execute a successful spike about half of the times they try. Getting a traffic ticket is another example—only occasionally does a policeman stop us for a driving error. Gambling is still another illustration, and the persistence of those who gamble is testimony to the strength of these schedules. Winning a bet, the positive reinforcement, occurs very seldom but nevertheless seems to be a strong enough reward to encourage continued persistence.

One important thing distinguishes fixed ratio from variable ratio schedules: with fixed ratio reinforcement, one knows precisely when reinforcement will occur and can anticipate it. As we noted with the elevator salesperson, one who is reinforced on this basis tends to pause after reinforcement before resuming the original rate of behavior. Since with a variable ratio schedule one doesn't know when reinforcement will occur, the person will produce the reinforced behavior at a more consistent rate, without pauses. This suggests that a variable ratio schedule is the one to use to elicit a steady and stable performance in another's behavior.

Furthermore, for a fixed total amount of reinforcement, a variable ratio schedule is more effective than a continuous or a fixed ratio schedule because it induces a longer lasting change in the frequency of the reinforced behavior. What does this mean? Let us say a child is given a dime after he or she completes every page of a reading assignment (continuous reinforcement schedule). A second child is placed on a variable ratio schedule in which the average frequency of reinforcement is one out of three times. To make the total amount of reinforcement for this second child equal to that of the first, this child is given 30 cents every time he or she is reinforced. If the children continue for about 90 pages with their corresponding schedules, they will both earn nine dollars. But even with total reinforcement being the same for both, the experimental findings suggest that the child who was trained with the variable ratio schedule will continue reading and will ultimately read more than the one who was trained with a continuous reinforcement schedule (Ferster & Skinner, 1957; Skinner, 1961).

Why is the variable ratio schedule more effective? One reason is that the person being trained is not certain when he or she will receive a reinforcer. Consequently, when reinforcement ceases, the person is not sure if there will be no more reinforcers or if there is simply an extraordinarily long delay. This uncertainty makes the person persist longer in producing the behavior, even though he or she is not reinforced. Another practical reason for using a variable ratio schedule is that it is not necessary to be present at all times to observe and reinforce, as it is when a continuous reinforcement schedule is employed; the variable ratio schedule also requires fewer reinforcers, which is helpful especially if the particular reinforcers selected tend to lose their luster with repeated use.

Finally, the variable ratio is the most subtle of the various schedules. At times it is better that people not make an explicit connection between the reinforcer they receive and their performance of specific behaviors. We hope to show some very legitimate bases for deliberately reinforcing behavior, but many people nevertheless object to the idea of being controlled or manipulated by another person, even if the change can be beneficial and despite the fact that social influence is a common aspect of social interaction, intentional or otherwise. The connection between reinforcement and the performance of certain behaviors is far more obvious with a continuous reinforcement schedule.

In general, then, where necessary a reinforcement schedule might start with continuous reinforcement, shift as soon as possible to a variable ratio schedule and gradually increase the proportion of nonreinforced to reinforced behavior. In this way, at final stages of training, the changes can be obtained with a very small amount of reinforcement.

Extinction

One other relevant term we need to mention is *extinction*, which is the return of a behavior to its original or prereinforcement level, or the gradual elimination of a new response (behavior change) through removal of the reinforcers. Examples may help to illustrate: little Polly likes to pull on the leaves of her mother's rubber plant. Her parents decide to punish her for damaging the plant by slapping her fingers. A respected friend sees them punishing Polly for touching the plant and suggests that "frequent physical punishment can inhibit spontaneity in children." The parents point out that their punishment had been effective because Polly now only rarely touches the plant; however, they decide to stop slapping her fingers. To their chagrin, they find that Polly gradually resumes her old habit of pulling on the leaves of the rubber plant. Her newer response, not touching the plant, was extinguished when the negative reinforcer ceased.

A second example relates to the development and elimination of a child's tantrum behavior. Some parents who are busy or under great pressure from other sources may tend, because of preoccupation, to overlook or ignore their children when they are "behaving," being forced to attend to them only when they misbehave or throw a tantrum. The parents' attention, since it is hard to come by, is reinforcing for the child and thus helps increase the frequency of, for instance, tantrums. Occasionally, the parents may even try to ignore the tantrum, but they may have to give in to the child just to stop the disturbance. In this case the tantrum is reinforced on a variable ratio schedule. Experiments have shown that a child's tantrum behavior can be extinguished by parents who stop attending to (and thereby stop reinforcing) such behaviors (Williams, 1959).

Negative Reinforcement

A final consideration about reinforcement is how to balance the use of (1) positive, (2) negative, and (3) positive-plus-negative reinforcers. We generally emphasize the application of positive rather than negative reinforcers, for several reasons. First, the effects of punishment are far more complex than the effects of reward or positive reinforcement. Punishment involves a variety of side effects that complicate a situation. For example, experimental findings have shown that when a person is punished in a given situation, although the behavior being punished decreases in frequency, there also develops a tendency to avoid the situation (Azrin & Holz, 1966). Thus a child who is punished in the classroom may begin to play hooky or feign illness to avoid returning to the painful situation.

Punishment may also result in aggression toward the punishing agent. Suppose a teenager is being punished and retaliates aggressively with the result that the punishment stops. The teenager's aggressive retaliation is reinforced because it is instrumental in stopping the negative reinforcement—the punishment. Thus, even if aggressive retaliation of this kind is only occasionally effective in stopping punishment, aggressive responses will be reinforced and will become more frequent.

It is interesting to note that this type of learned aggression is also supplemented by a reflexlike response that experimental studies have shown to occur quite automatically and indiscriminately whenever an organism is subjected to pain. For instance, animals placed in a cage suddenly attack each other when they are shocked by a current passed through the cage floor. This automatic aggression is vented toward anything or anybody in the immediate vicinity of the organism being punished (Azrin & Holz, 1966). Such aggressive responses following punishment are, of course, another reason that punishment is undesirable for use in social situations.

Although punishment can generally be avoided in influencing another's behavior, there are times when it becomes necessary. For this reason, we briefly note that under the following conditions, punishment *can* successfully and permanently suppress the occurrence of a behavior (Azrin & Holz, 1966): (1) when the person being punished can in no way avoid the situation; (2) when punishment is sufficiently severe in quality and is introduced and maintained at the same level of severity (rather than being introduced at a low level and gradually increased in intensity); and (3) when the punishment is administered on a continuous schedule of reinforcement immediately after the undesirable behavior occurs. As we see later on, however, the most effective use of punishment occurs when a person is simultaneously positively reinforced for some alternate and more desirable behavior.

Among the characteristics of punishment mentioned above, the most important seems to be its severity. Punishment of moderate severity does not produce lasting changes, whereas very severe punishment, administered on a continuous schedule, can and does. Our discussion of phobias in the next chapter helps explain this exceptional finding.

Still another form of punishment in social situations is merely the withholding or withdrawal of positive reinforcers and rewards. In one study, teenagers who were playing pool in a recreation room were punished for undesirable social behavior (quarreling, bumping one another, using abusive language) by being immediately removed from the recreation area and forced to wait alone in an isolated booth for 15 minutes (Tyler, 1965). This procedure, generally referred to as "time out," was found to be quite effective in minimizing undesirable behaviors in the recreation area and could be equally effective in any such situation.

The withholding of positive reinforcers, especially positive social reinforcers, is a frequent means of social control that most of us use intuitively (ignoring someone who is talking to us, not smiling when we greet someone). Systematic use of this technique in psychotherapy is illustrated by a situation in which the nurses on a ward ignore the "crazy" jumbled talk of a schizophrenic, attending to the individual only when he or she makes "normal" conversation. Such a technique—withholding attention—can minimize the frequency of the crazy talk. Even more importantly, when the mild punishment of withholding attention is combined with positive reinforcement of more desirable behaviors, even stronger effects can be obtained. The same patient will rapidly give up the crazy talk and increase normal conversation if it is being reinforced with cigarettes, food, or anything else he or she especially enjoys.

Positive Reinforcement

Although punishment is sometimes appropriate and effective, it is still preferable to rely on the use of positive reinforcers in most instances, as follows. To "change a person's behavior" in a given situation means to induce him or her to replace one activity in that situation with another behavior. So, in general, behavioral change involves diminishing the frequency of one action and increasing the frequency of another. In fact, change can often be conceptualized as occurring along a continuum, with the undesirable behaviors—those to be diminished in frequency—assigned to one end and the desirable behaviors—whose frequencies are to be increased—assigned to the other end. Thus, the process of change is a movement from one end of this continuum to the other.

Two examples show how this works. Beanie is a child who is uncooperative at times—he does not listen to his parents, refuses to help out with household chores, and so on. Implicit in the formulation of change in this case is the building of cooperative behaviors on Beanie's part. His continuum would show a high frequency of uncooperative behaviors and very low frequency of cooperative behaviors at one end, and a high frequency of cooperative behaviors and low frequency of uncooperative behaviors at the other end. Obviously, then, increases in cooperative behavior tend automatically to force decreases in uncooperative behavior, and vice versa. Given that fact, and knowing the desired direction of change, it would therefore be possible to accomplish the desired change either by focusing primarily on a decrease of the undesirable behaviors or on an increase of the desirable behaviors. To decide to use primarily positive reinforcers would mean to focus on an increase of Beanie's desirable behaviors rather than a decrease of his uncooperative ones.

A second example is Alphie, the "silent husband," who hardly ever discusses things with Bet, his wife. She construes his silence as coldness, lack of affection, and unwillingness to share his problems and concerns with her. Alphie's continuum would be formulated with a high degree of silence and low frequency of conversation about his life outside his home at one end, and at the other end, a low frequency of silence and a high frequency of such conversation. Now it is clear that inducing Alphie to talk more about what happens at work or what happens in his contacts with others during the day would automatically diminish the frequency of his silence. Here again, then, focusing on those behaviors whose frequency should be increased requires only positive reinforcers. The alternative procedure in both cases would be to diminish the undesirable behaviors through the use of negative reinforcers, a distinctly different approach.

Negative-Positive Reinforcement

Unfortunately it is not always possible to use only positive reinforcers with humans. There are certain situations in which the behavior being changed is so destructive and the amount of damage to oneself or others so great in only a brief period of time, that gradual change by reinforcement of desirable behaviors to replace the destructive one is simply not fast enough. In cases where there is a time pressure then, it becomes necessary to use both negative and positive reinforcers simultaneously, as follows. Negative reinforcers are used initially to bring about a sudden drastic limitation in the frequency with which the destructive behavior occurs. Positive reinforcers are used at the same time to bring about more desirable behaviors. For example, in some extreme cases of autism children might claw at their cheeks, eyes, ears, and so on, causing a great deal of physical damage to themselves in a short time. In such a case hospitalized children are frequently bound to a bed, thus completely disabled and prevented from hurting themselves. But tying children to their beds in no way promotes a constructive change. As an alternative, they are untied and given freedom to move and play except that through mild shock (administered via light electrodes that are attached to their arms) they are severely punished for reverting to their previous behaviors, such as any movements of their arms toward their faces. They actually have considerable freedom of movement and are provided with a variety of toys to play with. Since there is a possibility of eliciting a large number of behaviors that are not self-destructive, positive reinforcement can be used to increase and maintain these other more desirable behaviors, which, incidentally, counteract the destructive ones. In the meantime, shock continues to be available for curtailment of destructive behavior. This case then illustrates the joint application of severe punishment, to quickly lower the frequency of destructive behavior, with positive reinforcement of alternate and more constructive behaviors for the child.

To summarize, in the majority of cases where it is necessary or desirable to change another's behavior, it is possible to rely primarily on positive reinforcers. When positive reinforcers are used in this way, they increase the frequency of desired behaviors, thereby automatically decreasing the frequency of the undesirable behaviors. The remaining cases require simultaneous use of positive and negative reinforcers, as described above. The joint use of positive and negative reinforcers is effective in bringing about a desired change in such situations faster than could be achieved with positive ones alone. Finally, exclusive use of negative reinforcers at any time is generally discouraged —they are less effective and can create many troublesome social and ethical issues.

Recall that we have mentioned two criteria to look for when analyzing a problem situation: (1) the undesirable behaviors that are associated with distress and that seem to be beyond the control of the persons involved, and (2) the implied direction of change, or the desirable behaviors that would relieve the distress and frustration. Given the concepts of reinforcement, let us now add three more steps to help with further refinement in problem definition: (1) the reinforcers present in the situation that might be helping to maintain or even increase the undesirable behaviors, (2) other available reinforcers in the situation that might help to increase the frequency of desirable behaviors, and finally (3) the agents who might be used to administer these reinforcers.

To simplify matters somewhat, we have given names to the basic characters in our discussions. *Ragent* will identify the person serving as the Reinforcing AGENT, the one who initiates and reinforces changes in another. The PERson Being INfluenced will be known as *Prebyn*. Both names will be used throughout the remainder of the monograph so the reader can quickly identify the roles of the parties in the interactions.

SHAPING

One of Skinner's major contributions is his detailed description of the steps whereby reinforcers could be used to change the frequency of behavior (1961). These techniques are subsumed under the concept of *shaping*. To illustrate, suppose it is desired that a child be neater than he or she is. Should mother wait until the child has tidied his or her room to her satisfaction and then reinforce the child, or should mother initiate the change by altering the standard of her expectations? Experimental findings suggest that it would be most effective to proceed through a series of steps, positively reinforcing those behaviors that begin to approximate the desired end product more and more. To put it another way, one should positively reinforce the child's "good mistakes." Thus, any behavior that is slightly more tidy than usual should be enforced, but behaviors that are at a characteristic level of untidiness, or lower, should not be. Untidiness to mother may constitute not making the bed, not putting clothes away in the closet, not picking up toys, and being generally sloppy at the table. Some of these problems have several components; for example, being sloppy at the table may include all sorts of individual troublesome behaviors. If we were to observe any one of these irritating behaviors closely, we could specify a habitual level of untidiness in terms of number of offenses per day. There would be a fluctuation about this habitual level, of course—on certain occasions there would be less untidiness than on others. In shaping for tidiness, any improvement (a relatively lower frequency of untidy behaviors) would be reinforced immediately after it is exhibited, such as immediately following a meal at which the child has been slightly less sloppy than usual. The parents should ignore (not reinforce either positively or negatively) those occasions when the child's habitual level of sloppiness occurs or when he or she is even more sloppy than usual. Having reinforced the child a few times for being slightly less sloppy, the parents can then raise their standards and require even more tidiness before reinforcing. In this way the desired goal will gradually be attained.

One can perhaps see from the above example that keeping track of an intricate and extended shaping program could be much simplified by a careful recording of the gradual changes in the desired behavior (the one being manipulated) and the reinforcements given for those changes. Such a record can help determine, in accordance with the selected schedule, when to or when not to reinforce. We must know the exact frequency with which a certain behavior occurs before we can determine how to shape it. Keeping such a record provides realistic feedback; a picture of one's accomplishments and failures is thus an integral part of shaping techniques.

The use of shaping does not automatically exclude problems in which behaviors are abstractly defined. For example, we might wish that a certain person were more conscientious. To be "more conscientious" is an abstract summary of several problems involving specific behaviors. The use of shaping techniques relies on clear-cut definitions of an abstract issue in terms of its specific behavioral components. Therefore, if we wish someone were more conscientious, we must first define exactly what behaviors we would prefer that person to exhibit in different situations. Once those behaviors have been defined and quantified as to the frequency with which they already occur, a basis exists for employing shaping techniques. Other forms of this same problem are oft-expressed complaints such as these: "She doesn't give of herself," or "He's so cold, he never shows any feeling," and so on.

Shaping techniques may strike some as too analytical and calculating. The idea of initiating planned changes in another's behavior and actually keeping track of the progress in writing may at first glance appear offensive and dehumanizing. But in problem situations where these techniques could possibly bring about improvement, the choice seems to be the following: Either an individual can continue in his or her frustrated relationship with another person and express this frustration by negative feelings that may in turn perpetuate or even increase the distress (Beakel & Mehrabian, 1969), or the individual can seek to use some techniques for bringing about a change, so that he or she will feel more positive and be able to maintain a more fruitful association. It was interesting to see the changes brought about in a mother who had come to us feeling completely frustrated, helpless, and exasperated with her child. Following the use of reinforcing techniques, she began to get some feeling of mastery over what happened and was able to realistically observe and record improvements in the child's behavior. The parent was then able to express more positive feelings to the child, who in turn responded by being more cooperative.

In considering any changes induced through shaping, we must answer questions that may already have occurred to the reader: After the training period is over, and Ragent has obtained a desired change, and planned reinforcement stops—what happens? Does Prebyn revert back to the old ways? If so, what kind of shaping procedures minimize the possibility of a return to older habits and maximize the possibility that the new behavior will be retained?

Since use of a variable ratio reinforcement schedule induces the longest lasting changes, it is best to use this schedule from the beginning if possible, or at least to institute it at an intermediate stage. This is because a variable ratio schedule provides a more harmonious, that is, a less discontinuous, transition into the everyday situations where planned reinforcements are absent. Reinforcement may accidentally occur in such everyday situations and thus be consistent with the subject's expectations on the variable ratio basis, but if the subject has been led to expect continuous reinforcement, he or she is sure to be disappointed and may then cease to perform.

To illustrate, Muffy is a child whose behaviors are first shaped for greater productivity in her school classroom with a variable ratio schedule. When shaping is terminated, her parents, as well as her teacher, may socially reinforce Muffy's new skills by showing their pleasure over her progress with her schoolwork. But even more interestingly, there are many subtle rewards that may follow from Muffy's better school performance, such as (1) implied superiority among her peers, a very powerful reinforcer that, incidentally, is maintained as long as one continues to excel; (2) the parents' willingness to buy her interesting and intellectually challenging gifts, partially due to their increased evaluation of her as a competent and intelligent child; and (3) a possible tendency on the part of the parents and teacher to treat her more like a responsible adult rather than an irresponsible child, another powerful reinforcer in our culture.

Muffy's example helps to illustrate that part of the challenge in using reinforcement techniques is for a parent, teacher, or psychotherapist to select a direction for change that will be self-reinforced when the program ceases—that is, to shape behaviors that will continue to be reinforcing for an individual. The difference between an ingenious teacher or parent and an average one is not so much the latter's inability to select behaviors that might continue to be reinforcing and therefore be maintained, but rather the former's acuteness in perceiving and shaping those behaviors that have more than the average likelihood of being positively reinforced.

There are countless instances of lesser interpersonal problems in which we might effectively use shaping techniques to modify our own behavior. For instance, we might find reinforcement useful in improving our own study habits or trying to quit smoking (Keutzer, 1968). To shape our work or study skills, we could select reinforcers—food, recreation, or listening to music—and decide on a schedule of reinforcement that would be contingent on our productivity. We may decide that if we can keep up two or more hours of work we are entitled to a particular recreation, and then reward ourselves if we succeed. A good rule is to always select small, meaningful, positive reinforcers, which are very concrete and well-defined and which, again, will not lose their effectiveness with repeated use. In shaping a behavior that requires a great deal of effort, the best positive reinforcer would be one that also involves some relaxation, since relaxation in itself can be a positive reinforcer.

Shaping can also be used with considerable success to socialize animals or train pets. For example, one lady complained that she couldn't seem to housebreak her cat completely. He would sometimes use his litter box but just as often go in various parts of the house. She said that she had been patting the cat whenever he went in the litter box, but this had not worked. It was suggested that she think of some food that her cat was particularly fond of, and even keep him slightly hungry so as to make this food especially tempting. Since in this case the cat did produce the desired behavior, but not consistently enough, it was suggested that he be given a small amount of the favored food immediately after using the litter box. The timing of this reinforcement would, of course, depend on the frequency with which the cat went into the litter box; if it happened approximately twice a day, then he could be reinforced only that often. However, if visits to the box were very infrequent, the shaping could initially focus on behaviors of approaching the box, with the cat being reinforced for moving very close to the box, next for touching it from the outside, then perhaps for just spending some time in the box, and finally, only for actually using it.

As a final example for this section we will consider a situation that illustrates that reinforcement theory can be useful not only in overcoming existing problems, but also in determining courses of action for the future to maximize the effectiveness and productivity of the persons involved.

Suppose two men establish a partnership. One of them, Mr. Meadows, has considerable experience in the business they're starting, while the other, Mr. Greenfield, is, in truth, "green." Right at the beginning, Mr. Meadows has a choice of several approaches. He could promise Greenfield a very large reinforcer before he has done anything to help accomplish the goals. In contrast, if promises of benefits were to be made contingent on Greenfield's contributions to the project, they would serve as reinforcers to encourage effort on his part. In sum, wholesale prediction of the positive outcome of an enterprise is less constructive since it is not contingent on the partner's contributions. Moreover, an all-encompassing initial promise detracts from the effect of positive benefits when they do happen, since they have already been taken for granted.

INADVERTENT REINFORCEMENT OF UNDESIRABLE BEHAVIOR

Frequently, certain behaviors are maintained because they are being reinforced in a very subtle way. In some instances Ragent may employ split reinforcers: a negative verbal (explicit) communication about a behavior along with a positive nonverbal (implicit) communication about the same behavior that is strong enough to counteract the effect of the negative verbal comment. We have all used such split reinforcers: when a husband surprises his wife with a fur coat on her birthday, she may respond with, "You shouldn't have done that, we can't afford it," while the pleasure in her eyes is obvious; and parents often have trouble refraining from laughter while reprimanding a child because what he or she did was cute even if it was naughty. Experimental findings have shown that, in such instances, the facial expression or the intonation of speech tends to override what is said, so that the overall reinforcing quality of the message is positive (Mehrabian, 1971, 1972). Even in cases where the explicit and implicit reinforcements are given at different times, the negative reinforcements may be overridden by more frequent nonverbal communications of pleasure, amusement, or encouragement.

Although the inadvertent use of split reinforcers can be harmless (note the coy reaction to the fur coat) or even beneficial, there are times when its subtle quality can give it an insidious and damaging effect. The following situations illustrate such cases.

Parental Conflicts Vented on Children

Mr. and Mrs. Vine are in conflict with one another but do not dare, or are unable, to express their conflict or disagreements directly. Thus, while peace and good feelings appear to reign between them, either of them may use one or more of their children to vent a sense of frustration and aggression. Let's say that Vinette, one of the children, has a habit of being careless and breaking things and that this is particularly disturbing to Mrs. Vine. Mr. Vine explicitly discourages that behavior, by means of negative reinforcement, when it occurs in his wife's presence. But sometimes, simultaneously or soon afterward, he implicitly encourages Vinette by, for example, being amused by what she does. The nonverbal communication is subtle enough not to be detected by Mrs. Vine, but even if it were Mr. Vine could always deny the implication by reminding his wife of the explicit statement with which he chastised Vinette for her behavior. For instance, Mr. Vine might say angrily, "How many times have I told you not to get your mother upset in that way?" followed a few minutes later by, "Why don't we go out and take a walk while your mother is cooling off?" Vinette's apparently undesirable behavior is reinforced, since making her mother angry results in increased attention from her father. The positive reinforcement from her father outweighs the negative reinforcement of the chastisement. Thus, Vinette's undesirable behavior is shaped and maintained by Mr. Vine, to the distress of Mrs. Vine. Through this devious means of expressing hostility to his wife, Mr. Vine may be reinforcing a self-destructive or socially undesirable behavior in Vinette, since he may see the immediate effect on his wife but fail to see the long-range effects on his child.

This type of problem has been informally observed by persons working in family therapy situations and is one of the bases for the development of some severe kinds of psychopathology in children. The child in such cases is caught within a conflict and over many years is led to learn a series of undesirable behaviors that serve no realistic function but merely are vehicles for the expression of negative and hostile feelings between the parents.

Goal Orientation

People who, to one degree or another, try to avoid facing fearful and failure-producing situations are generally referred to as *low achievers;* those who deliberately try to conquer fears or difficulties are the *high achievers.* One of the characteristics that distinguishes high from low achievers is their relative emphasis on success and failure. Failure is especially painful for the low achiever while success is especially rewarding for the high achiever. This difference explains why a high achiever is more willing to persevere at a problem that might involve failure while a low achiever becomes discouraged and quits (Heckhausen, 1967).

How can we understand the development of these relatively stable high or low achieving tendencies in terms of learning theory? How does one learn to be more or less persistent in the face of possible failure? Such learning probably occurs during childhood or early adolescence. In a family where children are frequently encouraged and rewarded for their efforts at a difficult task, persistence would come to be seen as worthwhile and rewarding. In another family the parents may have impossibly high expectations for their children. The parents withhold gratification or reward until the children reach one of these major goals. The children might initially keep trying and actually succeed in small stages, but in the absence of reinforcers to encourage their small successes, persistence is extinguished. In yet another family, expectations might be minimal. The parents indulge and overgratify their children in every respect, reinforcing them whenever the opportunity arises, regardless of their activities. In this case the children would not have to work at or persist in developing skills in order to earn some of the rewards that most children have as they grow up (McClelland, 1961). When they finally move outside the family environment, they face a considerable handicap since they discover that rewards are no longer as readily available and that they greatly lack the skills to obtain the positive reinforcements they once had. This new situation is equivalent to being faced with unrealistically high expectations from others, and so the children learn to give up easily in the face of adversity.

Once such learning has occurred, either to achieve or not to achieve, we next ask how it is maintained. Why does a high achiever remain a high achiever and a low achiever continue to function as a low achiever? When high achievers continue to persist in the face of failure, eventually they succeed and therefore experience positive reinforcement on a variable ratio schedule. Such reinforcement thus encourages them further, and their pattern of persistence is maintained in a stable way. Low achievers, in contrast, are caught in a vicious cycle. They avoid any situations that have led to failure and thereby exclude for themselves any possibility of being rewarded for persistence. Thus they are never reinforced for positive accomplishments following initial failure; avoiding the noxious situation that led to the failure does provide some measure of reinforcement through relief. In this way, any situation that bears a hint of failure becomes, through generalization, a negative one to be avoided, and the low achieving pattern is maintained.

The implication of this analysis is that the learning environment created for low achiever types should be different from that created for high achievers. Low achievers initially need situations in which failure is very infrequent and where their efforts are often positively reinforced. They could gradually be exposed to more frequent failures as they attain mastery of a task. Learning should be presented to them not so much as a challenge but as an experience that is associated with cooperation and good feelings. It is not so critical for high achievers to avoid the experience of failure. In fact, without a sufficient amount of failure they may even lose interest. They therefore should have a learning environment in which challenge and competition are basic factors and where success and failure occur equally. Once we can understand the mechanisms by which people cope with problems, we can devise reinforcing techniques that depend on the stable differences among the individuals involved.

Psychosomatic Illness

Illness of any kind, physical or psychological, may come to be associated with positive reinforcements. Talk about being sick or even actual physical reactions can be shaped and maintained to a point where it is difficult to distinguish real illness from malingering (Brady, 1966). This may explain why escape through illness, either feigned or imagined, is becoming an increasing concern. Our assumption that physiological problems like headaches can be reinforced and modified is supported by experiments that show that physiological responses can be modified without even Prebyn's awareness that his or her reactions are being systematically changed (Brady, 1966; Engel & Hansen, 1967; Hefferline, 1959).

Children or adults may be given undue attention, sympathy, privileges, and relief from responsibility when they are sick, which could encourage them to resort to any number of minor symptoms of distress—headaches, nausea, aches and pains. These psychologically motivated illnesses serve as a means of escape from responsibilities and, furthermore, as a source of gratification and attention. For example,

"Davey, your father wants the lawn mowed this afternoon before the company comes tonight."
"My stomach hurts, Mom. I just don't feel very good."
"Well, dear, then why don't you go lie down and maybe your brother will do the lawn for you this time."

Another way to encourage the development of this pattern is for a parent to let a child stay home from school because "he needs more sleep today," or "she didn't get her studying done." When the child sees that his or her parents don't mind such small, but still socially unacceptable, evasions he or she will be inclined to use that type of release more often.

SPEEDING UP THE SHAPING PROCESS

One problem inherent to shaping techniques is that if we desire to change certain behaviors that someone spontaneously emits, then we must simply wait until that person produces some action in the direction of the desired change that can be reinforced. This makes the application of shaping somewhat awkward since it can be very time consuming and erratic at the initial stages. Therefore, it is important to find eliciting procedures that will encourage variations in the behaviors that are to be shaped. This section includes such a series of techniques to speed up the shaping process particularly during the initial stages.

Verbal Requests for Change

One possible approach is simply to *ask* a person to change, indicating the reward that can be expected for his or her efforts. However, when such a request is made, variability, either desirable or undesirable, is more likely to occur. Thus, in the case of one child, Quid, who had sloppy table manners, his parents could have waited without comment until he exhibited slight improvement and then gone on to shape the changes as indicated; or they could have communicated to Quid that they would like it if he were less messy. Let us imagine the alternatives. If his reaction is to comply somewhat with their request, then he is reinforced and shaping is initiated. But the child may well be initially defiant and produce even worse table manners than before. Such an increase is not cause for distress, however, because messiness would soon begin to return to its habitual level, and could thus be reinforced.

Modeling and Prompting

In a new or ambiguous situation where people do not know how to act, they often rely on others around them, imitating their behaviors. This imitation is known as *modeling* and it provides many additional opportunities to apply reinforcement techniques (Bandura, 1965; Bandura & Walters, 1963).

A typical situation is the consistent reinforcement of undesirable but "cute" behaviors: "That scatterbrain smashed up her car again," followed by amused laughter; "Foxie bluffed through his book report today. I shouldn't have laughed along with the students but his antics were really very funny"; or parents who giggle with their children when one of them spills milk in a restaurant. Other people in the environment—classmates, brothers and sisters, or whatever—observe that supposedly undesirable behaviors were not punished when they happened but rather became the source of attention and merriment. This makes the social role or model that is implicitly and consistently communicated to the child not only one to emulate but also one that is positively reinforcing. Consider the following example of self-image and identity development.

Tang's parents see a strong resemblance between his features and those of Uncle Elvin. In the child's presence they mention this resemblance occasionally, and of course bringing up Elvin often leads to comments on his characteristics, anecdotes about some of the things he used to do, and so on. As Tang grows up, then, he is frequently reminded that he is like someone else and also receives information about that person. He perhaps gets an impression from the conversations he hears that Uncle Elvin was quite an outstanding figure (whether for good or bad) and begins to act like Uncle Elvin in some of the more obvious and easy ways to model. As the parents and relatives notice some of Tang's increased resemblances to Uncle Elvin, their ideas of their similarities are further strengthened, and discussed. Thus the cycle repeats itself. Through this process, Tang gains a detailed picture of a person's attributes and experiences, is reminded to behave like that person, and is reinforced for doing so. The reinforcement goes as follows:

When Tang acts in certain ways that resemble Uncle Elvin, who was a rather significant figure for the relatives, he draws their attention and amusement—or possibly chagrin—becoming the center of attention. As he grows up he begins to take on more and more of Uncle Elvin's characteristics, a state of affairs that conforms to his parents' and relatives' expectations and provides him with a source of extra attention and reinforcement.

There are several important elements in the Tang-Uncle Elvin situation. First, when Tang lacks a repertoire of responses for a given situation, he is very susceptible to influence by models. The models may be other individuals whose behaviors Tang observes and emulates, or they may be roles that are verbalized by others as appropriate to that situation (or at least implicitly expected from Tang). In the examples we have considered, the circumstances are generally a question of what role to assume in life, that is, how to behave in various social settings. Naturally children have not established an identity as firmly as adults and are therefore more susceptible to any suggestions or guidelines that might be exemplified in others.

Second, persons in the environment of Prebyn somehow show an unusual preoccupation with either the model or the roles that they describe. That is to say, they talk about, attend to, or praise extensively either the models themselves or the roles associated with the models. This makes these particular models or roles salient aspects of the environment in which Prebyn functions. In the language of learning, these models are known as *discriminative stimuli,* because they are emphasized or set apart (discriminated) as special entities within rather complex situations —special because they signal reinforcement.

Third, any behavior of Prebyn's that resembles one of the model's tends to receive more emphasis from others than his or her other behaviors. In this way—through similarity with the behaviors of the model—a certain subset of Prebyn's behaviors is positively reinforced.

In short, the combination of a model (or a set of roles that correspond to a model) with reinforcement of any behaviors that emulate that model, can be an extremely powerful technique for shaping large sets of Prebyn's behaviors, particularly when he or she initially lacks a well-defined repertoire of behaviors.

The following experiment demonstrates the significant effect of using modeling to help children overcome their fear of dogs (Bandura, 1967). One group of children who were afraid of dogs had eight "parties" together, during which they received prizes and candy and watched another child, the model, play fearlessly with a dog. A second group had the same series of parties with the dog present but without any model who played with him. The results showed that a significantly greater number of children from the first group overcame their fear of the dog. Also, in testing sessions one month later, more of the children from the first group were willing to be alone in a playpen with the dog.

Rosen used a form of modeling to cure psychotic behaviors. One of his patients denied any psychotic behavior, claiming his real trouble was a spinal malformation and an extra bone in his back, which gave him an odd, springing step (Rosen, 1953). In the patient's presence, Rosen remarked offhandedly that he, too, had once had such a strange walking step, "when he was crazy." But when the patient tried to question him about his alleged symptom, he would talk of other things, ignoring the patient's wish to discuss the mutual problem. By pretending he was once psychotic and had experienced the patient's same symptoms, Rosen led his patient to see that the symptoms were gone and that Rosen was no longer crazy. The patient could thus view Rosen as a model—"If he got well, why shouldn't I, too?"

In using modeling, one must remember that people are more suggestible or malleable in unfamiliar circumstances. A model can then be a source of coping skills. Consider this application: If parents are attempting to teach a child a more regular set of working habits or a greater degree of persistence at solving problems, and if they have failed to elicit favorable behaviors in the child's habitual settings, they might temporarily use a new setting to encourage the new behaviors with modeling techniques. Thus, a vacation setting might provide parents an opportunity to set up a new kind of work-fun situation in which they exemplify ways to function that their child can copy or model. Any favorable response could then be reinforced and subsequently transferred (generalized) to their home environment.

While modeling refers to the process whereby elaborate sequences or complex sets of behaviors are imitated, *prompting* refers to the elicitation of one simple act. When we tell a child to "say dolly," we are using a prompt. If he says it we respond with "Good boy, good boy," and wait. If he spontaneously says the word again, we reinforce him; if not, then we prompt him again. Most parents use the prompt widely and intuitively with young children, accomplishing changes very quickly and subsequently reinforcing them positively.

Prompting or modeling can involve words or actions; nonverbal prompting techniques, as opposed to verbal ones, are usually more appropriate with adults than with children. It is easier and socially less awkward to prompt an adult with the use of nonverbal behaviors than to make an explicit request that may be denied, thus causing uncomfortable feelings for both parties. Explicit verbal requests for change need be used only when nonverbal prompts are not effective at all in initiating some variation in Prebyn's behavior.

Using a Third Party as a Model

So far we have discussed two sets of eliciting techniques: verbal suggestions or requests for change, and the use of prompts and models. A third technique is the indirect use, in Prebyn's presence, of a third person's behaviors as examples to be modeled. This is accomplished by specifically calling attention to those behaviors of the third person that are desired in Prebyn. You may have noticed this pattern with Tang and his Uncle Elvin. Although in that case the pattern occurred inadvertently, the method can, of course, be used deliberately. Suppose, for example, it is desired that Lyon, your son, practice his piano lessons more faithfully. His sister Dandi usually practices quite adequately without being told, so on those particular occasions when Lyon is present, Dandi can be reinforced with praise, or told, "Since you've been practicing so well, we'll get you the new sheet music you've been wanting." This technique draws Lyon's attention to the desired behavior and to the relationship between that way of behaving and a positive reinforcer. As a consequence, the likelihood that Lyon will practice more may increase.

You may have used this technique intuitively by pointing out to a friend some behavior of a third person, and saying something positive about it. In this way, without explicitly asking for a change, you drew attention to the desired behavior in a third person and also reinforced it. Implicitly at least, your friend received some communication about the desired behavior and witnessed some reinforcers that could occur consequent to that behavior. Of course praise and compliments are only one way to reinforce, and you might have chosen anything else which you knew your friend valued.

Following are some detailed illustrations of this same technique as it can be used at home or in school situations. Sometimes a teacher who is burdened with a large class of unmotivated students may find her- or himself attending only to those who are misbehaving in order to prevent their behavior from disrupting the rest of the class. One of the problems with orienting toward a misbehaving student is that attention from a teacher tends to be a positive reinforcer; chastising the student does not constitute a sufficiently negative reinforcer to offset the increased attention. One of the reasons that attending to a student reinforces the student positively is that, in a way, it communicates to the student that he or she has the power to control the teacher as well as the rest of the class. So if misbehaving wins the student attention and positive reinforcement, he or she will tend to maintain that same pattern in the classroom. This problem is so common that a number of techniques have recently been studied in an attempt to counteract it. One way is simply to ignore the misbehaving students while positively reinforcing those who are producing the required behaviors. Once again, according to the principles of shaping, the requirements for positive reinforcement would initially be set relatively low and then gradually increased as behavior improves. Initially the misbehaving students may become even more disruptive in trying even harder to elicit attention from the teacher, particularly if the teacher is one who previously attended to their misbehavior. However, if the teacher continues to ignore these disruptive behaviors they will tend to become less frequent.

It is easier for a teacher to initiate this technique with a new class than to change over to it in the middle of a school year. When from the beginning a teacher ignores misdeeds and positively reinforces desired behavior, increases in disruptive behavior are not expected from those students who have shown such tendencies in the past; the teacher in a way has presented a new kind of image vis-à-vis the class, and students quickly adapt to that role. They begin to perceive the teacher as someone who seems oblivious to "goofing off" antics but who offers much attention and recognition for positive actions.

Of course, the above classroom technique can be translated directly to family situations. Some parents drift into the habit of attending to their children only when they are being naughty or unruly, which forces the children to misbehave in order to be noticed by the parents. Here again, the parents have a choice between negatively reinforcing the behavior of a difficult child or positively reinforcing the good behavior of another child in the presence of the disruptive one. Positive reinforcement is the superior method, not only because it does not encourage negative behaviors through undue attention, but also because it creates a more positive relationship between parents and children. As we have already seen, when children perceive positive feelings they tend to reciprocate them, and when they receive them regularly they become even more manageable or more responsive to the parents' needs and desires.

The Token Economy

The earliest and most successful applications of reinforcement theory have occurred in those social situations where Prebyn is socially subordinate to and/or dependent on Ragent, such as the relationships of children to parents and teachers (Bijou & Baer, 1966), employees to employers, psychologically disturbed clients in a hospital to the hospital staff (Ayllon & Azrin, 1968; Buehler, 1966), and criminals or wartime prisoners to their prison staff (Holt, 1964). Control over privileges is a basis for devising some very powerful reinforcers (Bijou & Baer, 1966). Where the agents have almost complete control over at least the physical aspects of the environment, some dramatic changes in the behavior of large numbers of dependent individuals have been obtained. *Token economy,* so-called, is a reinforcement system that offers great versatility in many such settings (Ayllon & Azrin, 1968).

The token economy makes it possible to reward desired behaviors immediately with a token, a chip, or some other symbolic reinforcer. The system relies on two principles: (1) making clear the relationship between a reinforcer and a desired behavior can be more effective in behavior change than reinforcing without explanation; (2) humans and even some primates, such as chimpanzees, can be reinforced repeatedly and quite conveniently with some neutral object as long as they recognize that symbolic tokens can eventually be used to get actual material rewards, such as food, candy, or recreational privileges.

Individuals who understand speech should be told that if they produce certain desired behaviors they will be rewarded with chips, which in turn can be redeemed at certain times to obtain a variety of material reinforcers or privileges. For those who cannot understand speech, of course, the relationship between the behaviors to be reinforced and the tokens must remain implicit—that is, the first principle cannot be used. However, there is a technique for making the connection between symbolic and actual reinforcers. An animal subject or a retarded child, for instance, can be provided with tokens and placed in a situation with a model who can illustrate the value of the tokens. For example, the model may drop a token into a machine that produces a candy bar or a toy, which the model then enjoys in the presence of the child. At this point, if the child is provided with one or two tokens he or she usually imitates the model.

Once the significant relationship between the token and the other reinforcers is established, a graduated schedule is used to develop the child's ability to delay use of the tokens for longer and longer periods. One technique might require a single token for a candy bar at first, then two, three, four, and finally five. Or, the room in which tokens are exchanged for reinforcers may be open only certain times during the day, and so forth. The animal subject or the child is thus taught to appreciate a symbolic reinforcer and continues to see it as a reinforcer even when he or she must wait to cash it in.

The use of such token economies in state hospital wards has frequently brought on dramatic changes in the wards' social environments. Nurses and other ward attendants are provided with the tokens and detailed lists of desired behaviors that are to be shaped among the patients. The patients in turn are made aware of the relationships between the tokens and various privileges and rewards that the tokens will "purchase." Whenever a patient in the ward produces a desired behavior, any nurse or attendant who observes it can give an immediate and effective reinforcer. The desired behaviors may be a display of socially appropriate actions as opposed to "crazy" ones, a willingness to talk, cooperation with other patients in carrying out various duties on the ward, conversation that anticipates leaving the hospital and considers some of the realistic problems associated with life outside the hospital, and so on. In this way, the behaviors of large numbers of persons are shaped to approximate those of people outside the hospital setting, and therefore provide a basis for a graduated transition of the patients to their home environments (Ayllon & Azrin, 1968).

The methods of the token economy have obvious applications with children at home or in the classroom. Since there are numerous difficulties involved in using immediately available material reinforcers, an analogue of the token system can be used in which children collect points, consequent to certain of their behaviors, which apply toward subsequent reinforcement. In this way, the symbolic reinforcer can be used with much repetition and over several days. The delay period between the time a child receives the symbolic and the material reinforcers would of course depend on the level of the child's development; the interval would have to be much shorter for infants and children of two or three years than for a nine- or ten-year-old.

Kevin, a nine-year-old who was overweight, was informed that he could collect a certain number of points for losing weight, or for any other behaviors that contributed to loss of weight. A certain number of points were worth a certain toy or recreation. Kevin's parents helped to devise a shaping schedule for reinforcing his eating smaller quantities, or certain kinds, of food. Also, when at regular weighings the boy was found to have lost one pound or more, he received a certain number of points. The biggest reinforcers were designed to come from actual loss of weight, but component behaviors that contributed to loss of weight were also shaped. Some of the material reinforcers selected were a toy airplane which he had wanted for a long time, visits to a park where he could fly his airplane, or permission to stay out an hour later than usual to play with a friend. As in other instances of change, Kevin's achieved weight loss was a continued source of positive reinforcement in and of itself since he was able to participate more in sports and was generally more popular at school.

ADDITIONAL REINFORCEMENT TECHNIQUES: SATIATION, NEGATIVE PRACTICE, AND GROUP REINFORCEMENT

Satiation

Satiation is used to diminish the value of a reinforcer. For example, even if eating is positively reinforcing, it ceases to be so after we are full (or satiated). The satiation method in most cases involves the repeated use of a positive reinforcer to such an extent that it becomes negative. Almost all of us, on some occasion in childhood, have taken undue advantage of the opportunity to indulge in a favorite food, say banana cream pie, with the result that even the mention of banana cream pie was repulsive for many months thereafter.

This technique can have applications for overcoming some undesirable recurrent behaviors, such as smoking. A smoker could be induced to smoke at a much higher rate than usual, until satiation occurs and the smoking begins to be negatively reinforcing. Then the smoker can be required to continue smoking even longer at a relatively high rate until smoking could no longer be tolerated. This procedure may take several three- or four-hour sessions, and can be done in groups (Keutzer, 1967, 1968). Given the presently available evidence, it is difficult to say what the long-range effects of this technique are on different kinds of smokers. It is possible that the technique is more effective with infrequent smokers, like those who smoke socially but not necessarily when they are under stress. In general, development of methods for stopping the smoking habit will probably have to start with a characterization of types of smokers and proceed from there to the development of different techniques to counteract the smoking habit of each type.

Unfortunately, although it has been used quite successfully in hospital settings with severely maladjusted persons, the satiation technique for inducing behavior change has not been explored with unhospitalized persons. For example, one hospital patient hoarded towels in her room and also carried many around at all times by wrapping them around her arms and torso. She was induced to give up her hoarding behavior through satiation (Ayllon & Azrin,

1968). For several days nurses took towels to her room, handed them to her and left. The patient was initially delighted to receive the towels, but as their number increased she began to get more and more upset, and finally demanded that they be removed from her room. When the number of towels in the room exceeded 600 she began to take them out herself. Here then, through satiation, the positive reinforcer, a towel, was made negative and a lasting change in the patient's behavior was obtained. Subsequent to this satiation session, she kept an average of only two towels in her room.

Negative Practice

In another similar technique, *negative practice,* certain recurrent undesirable behaviors such as tics can be made even more negatively reinforcing so that they are ultimately discontinued (Ullmann & Krasner, 1969). A person is asked to practice the "involuntary" tic in front of a mirror. Of course, at first the person may not be able to reproduce an exact copy of the tic, but with practice is able to do so. The practice accomplishes two things. Being required to repeat one-hour practice sessions about twice a day requires effort and is therefore negatively reinforcing. Furthermore, the practice, which is aimed at an exact repetition of the tic, brings a so-called involuntary behavior under voluntary control. The end result, then, is a voluntary behavior that is negatively reinforcing; therefore it is discontinued.

Chronic headaches that are not biologically determined can sometimes be brought under control in the same way. People who suffer from headaches are advised to practice the headache for one hour every day. They are told to set aside a convenient time, find a place where they can remain undisturbed for that period, and try to make themselves get the headache during the entire hour of practice.

Typically, the result of such practice is that the patients discover what shoulder, neck, or facial muscles are becoming tense during the headache. In this way, once again, a seemingly involuntary reaction is brought under voluntary control.

Group Reinforcement

A person who is in charge of a group can minimize his or her own involvement as the primary reinforcing agent and also his or her sole responsibility for the effectiveness and productivity of the interrelated activities of group members. A group reinforcement technique has been found quite effective in helping to "spread around" this responsibility for overseeing and reinforcing each person's work in the group. In contrast to reinforcement of each individual's behaviors, this technique makes reinforcement contingent on the entire group's performance.

Teachers who have to deal with unmotivated groups of students frequently encounter serious disciplinary problems. Such students might be told that if they all stay reasonably quiet during class, they will be allowed five minutes of free time at the end of the period. Two aspects of this technique require consideration. First, the reinforcement, the five minutes of free time, is explicitly made contingent on good behavior during the rest of the class period. Second, and perhaps more interestingly, the reinforcement is also contingent on the coordinated efforts of the entire class. The advantage of this is that the resources of the group are used to exert social pressure. That is, if the reinforcement is worthwhile to the group, then the one or two troublesome members who jeopardize it may become the target of the group's disciplinary actions instead of requiring controls from the teacher. In this way the group's own reinforcers are used effectively to regulate each member's behavior.

More generally, when the behavior of a large number of people is to be influenced, it is very probable that some of these people will not respond to the selected positive reinforcers. If the cooperation of the entire group is necessary to perform a task and if one or two of the members get out of line, the whole function of the group will be disrupted. Therefore the group can be induced to exert control on those individuals who jeopardize the group's reinforcement, in order to safeguard group goals. The movie *The Dirty Dozen* illustrates this technique very clearly. Twelve criminals were promised freedom (a very positive reinforcer) for succeeding at a certain military task that required the cooperative efforts of the entire group. At various stages of their mission, group members positively reinforced each other's successes while negatively reinforcing others who were about to jeopardize the project. The intervention required from the officer in charge of the group was minimal.

In most situations, then, where several persons are involved in a project, a group reinforcer can be quite effective because it minimizes the authoritarian role of the group leader and generates more responsibilities among group members. The technique may be quite suitable in a family situation where several children are involved and may also have some interesting applications in hospital wards. In addition, it can be useful in somewhat rigid or bureaucratic settings where the focus of the individual tends to become so limited to his or her own role that the individual fails to see his or her relationship to others in the same organization. Very large groups, where it becomes too difficult for group members themselves to influence each other's behavior, can be broken down into smaller units, each under the direction of a group leader who is in turn part of a "group leader unit." The performance of each of these units may then be maximized with the use of the above technique.

SUMMARY

Change is seen to be a function of positive and negative reinforcers. For the most part, the kinds of change we have considered here are most amenable to the use of positive reinforcers. Furthermore, the process of change is a gradual one, involving small steps in the desired direction rather than large and discontinuous jumps. Therefore, one first determines the desired result and then rewards behaviors that increasingly resemble this result. In other words, Prebyn is reinforced for the "good mistakes" rather than for perfect performance all in one shot.

Since social influence relies heavily on the use of reinforcers, the effectiveness of shaping and related methods of behavior modification are largely dependent on Ragent's ability to find the appropriate rewards for Prebyn. In fact, the primary limitation of the techniques is the difficulty in finding reinforcers that fulfill two conditions: using them repeatedly (1) does not induce satiation, but continues to be rewarding to the person receiving them, and (2) does not deplete the resources of the one who is offering them. Satiation can be prevented by introducing a variety of reinforcers and shifting to variable ratio schedules as shaping proceeds, or by replacing material reinforcers with social ones.

Variable ratio schedules of reinforcement elicit a high rate of response from Prebyn and are the most resistant to extinction. They also permit the smoothest transition away from deliberate reinforcement, since they most resemble real-life situations. In considering change brought about in a controlled environment, one must also anticipate the likelihood that the new behaviors will persist even when planned reinforcement stops. Learning a new skill that is reinforced in many social situations will eventually make it unnecessary for the original teacher or guide to be present.

Not only can the principles of reinforcement help us bring about positive solutions to problems; often they can explain how certain problem behaviors began in the first place. Among these latter situations are a child's tantrums or a person's chronic underachievement. Finally, psychosomatic illness, suicidal talk, or other bizarre behavior can often be analyzed in terms of the inadvertent but occasional reinforcement of the problem behaviors.

In its initial stages, shaping can be speeded up in several ways. One can tell Prebyn what is required and how he or she will be reinforced for certain behaviors. Or one can use models whose behaviors are reinforced in Prebyn's presence. Token economies illustrate both of these and have been used successfully in hospitals and other settings that can be carefully controlled. Token economies also use symbolic reinforcers such as chips or points. Symbolic reinforcers are preferred over material ones because they can be delivered as soon as the desired behavior occurs. Moreover, they help to build one's capacity for delaying gratification, because the immediate but symbolic reinforcer must be "cashed in" later.

Another technique based on reinforcement principles is satiation: Prebyn is given so much of a reinforcer that he or she tires of it. This method is used to help Prebyn overcome an excessive desire for something that may ultimately be harmful (such as cigarettes). Negative practice is a method used effectively to counteract involuntary behaviors and states such as tics and headaches. A final method is group reinforcement, in which reinforcements to members of the group are contingent on the total group's integrated performance. Not every member of the group need be individually supervised, and development of leadership within the group is encouraged. People work cooperatively rather than independently, and disruptive members are controlled from within, thus freeing the group leader from the role of punitive agent.

The stimuli in our surroundings influence our behavior; thus, by inducing planned modifications in these stimuli we can obtain the desired changes in behavior, whether it be others' or our own.

Chapter 3

CREATING ENVIRONMENTS
CONDUCIVE TO CHANGE

CONDITIONING

We now consider some ways in which we can control our own or another's behavior by modifying the arrangements or sequences of stimuli that are likely to influence those behaviors. The general effects of stimuli on behavior must be considered before changing environments to influence behavior can be discussed.

Every stimulus elicits a response; thus every behavior could be seen as a response to some stimulus. This relationship is easily observed in the case of certain almost reflexlike responses to various situations. Fear and its physiological concomitants in reaction to threatening stimuli, or salivation in response to desired foods, and so forth, illustrate unconditioned responses. But there are also countless stimuli that do not automatically elicit the same response from everybody. How can we understand the reasons that different people react differently to the same stimuli? The answer to this can be found in the history of co-occurrences of certain pairs of stimuli in each person's background.

The Russian psychologist Pavlov observed that when dogs were consistently presented with food and this event was accompanied by the ringing of a bell, the dogs eventually could be made to salivate by the ringing of the bell by itself. Somehow, pairing the bell with the food had transferred some of the properties of the food to the bell, such that the bell could elicit salivation.

This process involves an unconditioned stimulus, food, which elicits a certain response, salivation. The food is then paired with a conditioned stimulus, the bell. Through this association, the bell begins to elicit the same response, salivation. To "condition" a response, then, means to present a stimulus that does not at first elicit the response, and follow it regularly with the unconditioned stimulus, which does produce that response, until eventually the conditioned stimulus alone comes to elicit the response.

Let us briefly summarize these terms. There are unconditioned and conditioned stimuli. Unconditioned stimuli are those that, in the absence of any learning, elicit a characteristic response; for example, shock elicits pain. Conditioned stimuli, however, are those that begin to elicit a particular response only after learning. The kind of learning in question is called conditioning: if we repeatedly pair a new stimulus with one that has in the past elicited a certain reaction from a person, this new stimulus alone eventually begins to elicit that same reaction.

It follows from these concepts of conditioning that every behavior is elicited by a certain stimulus, unconditioned or conditioned. In the presence of that stimulus the behavior occurs; in its absence the behavior does not occur.

Stimulus Generalization

Let us now consider an additional aspect of conditioning. In the case of the bell, the dogs could be conditioned to a tone of a certain frequency (pitch). Upon hearing that tone, the dogs would salivate. But would it make any difference if we changed the pitch upward or downward? Experiments have shown that the closer the pitch of the new bell to the one that was used originally, the more similar the response. In this case, as the pitch becomes increasingly dissimilar to the conditioned one, the incidence of salivation becomes less frequent. This phenomenon is termed *stimulus generalization:* when any stimulus elicits a response, stimuli that are similar to it also generally elicit that response. The more similar to the original one, the more likely it is to elicit that response. Thus, when a response is measured in terms of its intensity, the greater the dissimilarity between any stimulus and the conditioned one, the less will be the amount of the response.

Stimulus generalization, then, explains how, when a person has learned a response to a given stimulus, he or she produces it not just for that particular stimulus but for a series of others like it. The "catch," of course, is that a person may sometimes generalize a newly learned response too far, by reacting to some similar stimulus with the newly learned response when it is not really appropriate. A familiar example is a young child who is frightened by a neighbor's dog. Because of stimulus generalization, the child thereafter becomes afraid of all dogs.

Discrimination Learning

The process used to teach someone to counteract excessive generalization is known as *discrimination learning.* The subject is taught to respond differently to two stimuli that are within the same class but that differ in intensity, or some other quality. In the case of the dogs, a tone of a high pitch may be conditioned to feeding and one of lower pitch conditioned to shock. The animal quickly learns to salivate in response to the high-pitched tone and to lift his foot up to avoid shock in response to the low-pitched tone. The next question is, how far does each of these two tones generalize? The animal will respond appropriately until we select tones very close to the middle of the range between the low- and high-pitched tones, at which point he will become confused. In the same way, people can be taught to counteract generalization by learning to respond differently to various ranges of any particular stimulus.

Let us see how these concepts of conditioning are applied. Have you ever wondered how a person acquires an intense dislike for a certain food, color, or situation? Dislike for a food may have been acquired during a single experience when perhaps one ate the food while feeling sick, or while experiencing extreme emotional distress, such as an unusual argument in the family. The reactions that were elicited by the unpleasant stimulus (illness, distress in the family) became associated with the food, thereby transferring negative reaction to the food. Through generalization similar foods also come to be disliked. Sometimes, too, it could be a simple case of eating spoiled food, which elicits a negative response. Thereafter the dislike is generalized to that food and others similar to it. Intense dislike for a particular color or any other object can come about in much the same way.

The following case illustrates one of the variety of situations in which conditioning can be used to induce change (Eysenck, 1960). Oedipus, a boy of 10, would frequently wake up frightened in the middle of the night and run to his parents, wanting to get into bed with them. His parents had tried different methods to change his behavior but had been unsuccessful. Their lack of success may have been due to an unsystematic use of positive or negative reinforcers. On one occasion when Oedipus was forbidden to come into his parents' room, he spent four hours crying outside the door. As this problem persisted it created several difficulties and tensions in the family.

Oedipus was brought to a behavior therapist, who first established that his behavior was due to his fear of being alone in his own bed. Next the therapist attached electrodes to Oedipus' arm and asked him to imagine himself in his mother's bed and to say aloud, "Mother's bed." Just as he said it, he was shocked mildly. Then he was asked to say, "My bed," for which he received no shock. These two steps were repeated several times until the idea of being in his mother's bed became associated with an unpleasant emotional response, while the idea of being in his own bed was associated with relief from the unpleasant response. This simple application of conditioning principles was effective—Oedipus stopped disturbing his parents at night, and a number of related difficulties within the family were resolved.

One might object that Oedipus was merely conditioned not to think about being in his mother's bed and that the physical response of getting up and crying at the door in the middle of the night was something different and could persist. The relationship between the thought of being in mother's bed and actually approaching mother's bed is understood in terms of the concept of stimulus generalization. In fact, the effectiveness of the method hinges on stimulus generalization: the thought of being in mother's bed is conditioned to be negative, and actually being in mother's bed also becomes negative, through generalization. If difficulty had been encountered, then generalization could have been facilitated either (1) by using a more painful stimulus in the conditioning, or (2) by negatively conditioning thoughts and actions that approximated, in increasing degrees, the actual behaviors of Oedipus.

STIMULUS CONTROL

Stimulus control is another application of conditioning. It is based on the idea that individual responses are conditioned to, or associated with, specific stimuli; the occurrence of a particular stimulus consistently triggers a certain response. An obvious implication here is that if we desire certain behaviors to occur more often in the future, then we must create a stimulus environment that is conducive to the occurrence of those behaviors; or to diminish undesirable behaviors, we need an environment that will elicit responses other than the undesirable ones. Stimulus control can help us change our own behavior as well as that of others.

Before psychoanalysis, doctors would prescribe rest and a vacation for anxious patients whose physical condition did not account for their psychological distress. Such advice can be seen as an application of stimulus control. A restful and pleasant environment elicits both behavioral and physiological responses that differ from tension and anxiety, and thus could at least bring about temporary relief.

Dieting

Many Americans have difficulty regulating their diets due to an abundance of food and a low level of physical activity. Stimulus control might be of great assistance in regulating eating. For example, suppose most eating is done at home. If a specific diet is being used, stocking only the permissible items can be a critical factor in the success of the diet. If a person can limit food purchases to only the "skinny" foods that are permitted, then he or she would have to make a special trip to the store to transgress, or consume the forbidden foods in a restaurant or someone else's home. All these alternatives require more effort than simply reaching into the refrigerator to get a forbidden item. Thus, exercising control for a short time, while shopping, makes dieting easier in the long run by eliminating the temptations to indulge.

"But," you might object, "this applies only to those living alone, and many, if not most people who live alone probably do not eat most of their meals at home. Isn't there some modification of the 'food stocking' technique for those whose families like lots of 'goodies' in the cupboard?" The goodies are usually consumed by children who can afford to be less concerned about dieting. But they would probably be more than happy to consume their goodies to the point of satiation in the neighborhood drugstore or ice cream parlor. Single people who eat in restaurants can use the somewhat less effective modification of the basic technique given below.

It is further possible to control the desire to purchase the forbidden foods while shopping. Hunger is the key determinant here—it is a stimulus of overwhelming impact in determining not only what we eat but also what we buy. It generates certain not-to-be-ignored response patterns. The food-purchasing behaviors of a hungry person are much more likely to sound like "I love this, I'm going to buy some" (a set of responses to hunger learned in the past), than "This is good for me whether I like it or not, so I'll buy it" (a more recent dietetic restriction on established likes and dislikes). If the immediate and demanding influence of hunger is absent, then it is easier for the more rational dietetic limitation to take precedence in determining the purchases we make. It might therefore be wise for the person on a diet to go shopping right *after* a meal rather than before. (Incidentally, this can be suggested as good policy for economy-minded housewives as well, even if their families aren't dieting. It makes a surprising difference in the food bills.)

If controlling our stimulus environment for eating at home can be frustrating and difficult, it is even more of a problem when we are visiting others or dining out. People who typically eat in a variety of environments, therefore, must use slightly different versions of the above technique. For instance, rather than ordering a meal as is, with the good intention of ignoring the fattening elements (the baked potato, the hot buttered rolls), one can simply request that the waiter not bring those things to the table. The dieter is then structuring the immediate environment as much as possible to avoid the potent temptation of seeing forbidden foods in front of him or her. Controlling meals in restaurants, however, is more limited in scope and effect than the instance where the foods made available in the home are carefully selected. The greater limitation in the restaurant is that structuring of the environment is required on each eating occasion, whereas at home a single shopping trip can influence many eating occasions. Thus, it is generally preferable to design situations that more frequently exert influence on the behaviors in question.

There are three general guidelines for the use of stimulus control: (1) arranging an environment in advance to influence the occurrence of certain behaviors (Terrace, 1966), (2) doing this arranging on as broad a level as possible to exert the most influence with the least effort, and (3) arranging the environment when the related internal stimuli (feelings) are minimal. This third guideline allows the arranging to be done in terms of a predetermined plan rather than by strong feelings that automatically lead to certain of the undesirable behaviors.

Sleeping

Stimulus control might also be useful with children who have difficulty going to sleep. Sometimes children of five or six "can't sleep" when they go to bed but talk to their siblings, return to the living room to see the parents, or request a drink of water. If children share their bedroom with other children, or with toys and other stimuli typically associated with play and waking activities, the environment will discourage sleeping. It may be effective to isolate the children in a separate room that contains minimal cues related to daytime activities—no toys and no brothers and sisters who might elicit behaviors that prevent settling down to sleep.

RECIPROCAL INHIBITION

In their classic experiment, Watson and Rayner presented "little Albert" with a white rat and followed the presentation with a sudden, loud noise from behind that frightened him (1920). After this sequence was repeated only seven times, Albert was terrified of the rat by itself. This experimentally induced phobia generalized to other furry animals as well, such as rabbits or cats.

Such a phobia can be removed by placing the child in a high chair in anticipation of eating. The child is then shown a rat or other small animal at close range, which, of course, elicits considerable fear. Next the animal is moved far enough away so that it is still in view, but the child's fear is attenuated. Then the child is fed. During the feeding the animal is gradually moved closer to the child, the approach being gauged by the child's fear response (keeping it to a minimum). During the final step, the animal is placed on the child's table during the meal, and the child touches and plays with the animal without being anxious at all.

How can we understand this whole process—the induction and removal of a phobia? The induction, of course, was a simple case of conditioning—a furry animal was repeatedly paired with a loud noise until the animal alone produced the fear response. Stimulus generalization would then explain why the child might come to fear other similar small animals. Also, an unrealistic, maladaptive fear can be perpetuated because the person avoids the feared object as much as possible and thus has no opportunity to learn any new responses.

The development and maintenance of phobias can be explained as follows. Phobic avoidance of an object is reinforcing because it reduces fear. Thus, the sequence of development in a phobia is, for example, seeing an animal, experiencing some degree of reinforcement for successful avoidance—the reduction of fear. In this pattern, avoidance is shaped and maintained. With no guidance from others, then, Prebyn completely avoids the animal or situation that he or she fears and does not learn that it is harmless. Such intense fear reactions, often conditioned to quite harmless entities, are frequently observed in clinical and experimental settings and were quite resistant to change until the following techniques were developed.

Reciprocal Inhibition

The technique of *reciprocal inhibition* has been found to be successful in counteracting such fears (Wolpe, 1958, 1969). It requires a response (such as eating) that can inhibit the occurrence of the maladaptive response (such as fear). This technique was illustrated in the case above, where the eating minimized, or directly inhibited, the possibility of anxiety and fear because the pattern of autonomic (physiological) reaction associated with eating inhibited the autonomic reaction associated with fear and anxiety. This direct inhibition weakened the link between the feared object and the fear response, while simultaneously strengthening the link between the feared object and the relaxed and comfortable response.

The inhibition of the physiological responses associated with anxiety, due to eating, or conversely the inhibition of relaxation associated with eating, due to anxiety, is the basis for the name of the technique—reciprocal inhibition.

If relaxation and anxiety can inhibit one another reciprocally, then how can we be sure that relaxation will win over anxiety, rather than the other way around? To insure success, a situation is designed in which anxiety is initially very weak, as was the case in the child's gradual exposure to the feared rat.

If we had presented the child with a continuous strong dose of the feared object by leaving the rat right in front of him or her, the fear would have been too intense for relaxation and eating. Thus the child was first reminded of the fear by seeing the animal at close range, but it was then removed to a distance that diminished its threat. The relaxation associated with eating then helped the child counteract the weak fear that might have remained at that distance. Thus, the new response of relaxation was conditioned to the object while it was distant, and as it was moved closer the child continued to maintain a state of relaxation, through generalization. In this way the conditioned reaction of fear was gradually and completely removed.

There are many behaviors that can be used to directly counteract, or inhibit, the occurrence of anxiety. These include physical activity (preferably strenuous); self-assertion through mild expression of negative feelings toward another ("standing up for your rights"); and relaxation, which can be induced through eating, deep breathing, muscle exercises, or perhaps tranquilizing drugs (Jacobson, 1938). Incidentally, the relaxation induced by eating may also increase the possibility of friendly and conforming reactions. The businessman's habit of negotiating over lunch is more than mere convenience.

Areas of Application for Reciprocal Inhibition

It has been suggested by some behavior therapists that unrealistic fears or anxiety reactions are the essential basis of any neurotic or maladaptive behavior. If this were the case, then it would follow that all neurotic behaviors could, in principle, be treated with reciprocal inhibition. Rather than debate the validity of this conception of neuroticism for *all* cases, we will simply accept it as correct for a great many cases and will examine in some detail the application of reciprocal inhibition to a variety of situations. The techniques involved are useful, quite simple, and easy to apply.

Linda was a little girl who, within the course of two or three weeks, saw a friend fall into a swimming pool and drown, lost another friend who died of meningitis, and witnessed a car accident in which one person was killed. She somehow associated these traumatic experiences with the absence of her mother at those times, and subsequently the absence of her mother elicited very strong anxiety reactions from Linda. Linda's therapist, after having established the cause of her fears, asked her to lie down, close her eyes and then imagine being separated from her mother for just five minutes. As the therapist helped Linda to vividly imagine this situation, she was in a very relaxed state, and the relaxation helped to counteract or inhibit the anxiety stemming from the imagined separation. She was gradually led to imagine longer and longer periods of separation, but always while in a relaxed state. Following several sessions of this procedure, Linda no longer feared being away from her mother. As in the case of Oedipus, the effectiveness of Linda's cure hinged on stimulus generalization —from imagining separation from her mother to actually being separated from her.

The above technique involves inducing a subject to relax and imagine some weak but analogous version of the conditioned stimulus that elicits anxiety. Others involve hypnotizing the subject and presenting to him or her as vividly as possible the various stimuli that increasingly resemble the conditioned stimulus that is feared.

When a person is so extremely anxious and agitated that use of the simple relaxation techniques does not appear possible, relaxation might be physiologically induced with tranquilizing drugs. In one case, a boy who was terrified of animals in general was given sedation for three days. Once he was relaxed because of the sedation, he was gradually exposed to various animals until he overcame his phobia.

Another case history report involves Ted, a child who became terribly frightened of any moving vehicles after having been in a car accident. He was helped with the relax-through-eating technique. For Ted food was used both as a reward for talking about cars initially and as a means of inhibiting his anxiety.The therapist began by making conversation with Ted. After they had become acquainted and Ted was adjusted to the surroundings, the therapist briefly and casually mentioned something about traveling. Ted had been so upset and frightened that even talk about cars or moving vehicles of any kind had previously displeased him, so when he responded to the therapist's conversation by talking about a car, he was immediately rewarded with some chocolate. Once his talk about cars was reinforced positively, he began to talk of them more frequently, and the therapist continued to reinforce him with chocolate. Eventually Ted and his therapist were able to play games with toy cars and even have accidents with them—Ted eating chocolate all the while. They next progressed even further to sitting in a stationary vehicle, with Ted still eating chocolate. The next step was to make a brief trip to the store (eating more chocolate). Finally, after gradually taking longer trips, Ted overcame his fear of cars and traveling completely. Throughout, the candy served both as a reinforcement to encourage Ted's increasing involvement with cars, and as an inhibitor of his anxiety reactions.

Forced Exposure

There are some situations that do not require a direct inhibition of an anxiety reaction, in which fear can be overcome by merely forcing a person into the presence of a feared object.

We have already noted that one prime reason for the maintenance of an irrational fear reaction is that the person learns to anticipate and avoid the feared object, thereby never realizing that the fear is irrational. Joseph Wolpe, one of the major proponents of reciprocal inhibition, conducted some experiments with cats that are of interest at this point. He first placed them in a cage and shocked them by passing a current through the cage floor. Whenever the cats were placed on the cage thereafter, they exhibited a fear reaction that persisted for several months, even though they were not shocked again. In this case where the initial stimulation was probably quite painful, merely forcing the cats into the presence of the feared stimulus was not sufficient to alleviate their fear of it (Eysenck, 1960).

Another researcher, Guthrie (1935), suggested that if somehow, perhaps accidentally, a subject could be induced to produce a different response in the presence of the feared stimulus, then the second response would be retained until further new learning occurred and a third response was associated with the object. Guthrie called this a process of one-step learning and illustrated it in a large number of situations, one of which was the taming of wild horses. When a horse is mounted for the first time, it reacts violently. But if the rider can stay on top of the horse long enough, the animal changes dramatically and produces a novel set of reactions to the same stimulation, and those reactions are maintained without any recurrence of the initial disturbance.

Another way to understand such dramatic changes is that the anxious or disturbed condition is in itself negatively reinforcing for Prebyn, so if he or she can be forced to stay in a situation where there are actually no adverse consequences, then those disturbed behaviors that are negatively reinforcing will quickly diminish in frequency (Stampfl & Levis, 1967).

Wolpe's results with the cats might discourage one from hoping to achieve change with the use of forced exposure such as Guthrie suggested. But working with human beings does seem to provide a basis for change through forced exposure—change that can include successfully overcoming maladaptive and unrealistic fears. Let us consider an example.

Since snake phobics are relatively common, they have been the object of many experiments in the area of reciprocal inhibition. One of these involved fitting the phobic with electrophysiological equipment to directly measure heart rate, blood pressure, and perspiration. When induced by the experimenter to hold a harmless snake, the physiological indicators showed a very sudden and drastic increase in anxiety. But within a short time the anxiety subsided to normal levels. In other words, holding a snake just briefly is sufficient to overcome the fear. Such a procedure would of course hinge on the experimenter's ability to induce the phobic to hold a snake. If he or she fails to do so the experimenter could resort to the technique of desensitization, which is considered in the following section.

Although there is not much actual experimentation with direct confrontations with the feared object, a related technique (*implosive therapy*) has shown promising results (Stampfl & Levis, 1967): Prebyn is asked to vividly imagine and describe a feared object as elaborately as possible. In this imaginary situation, he or she encounters the aversive stimulus repeatedly without any negative reinforcement from that stimulus itself. In addition to the reason already mentioned, there is another explanation for the success of forced exposure or implosive therapy: the repeated practice of one's own distress in a harmless situation becomes negatively reinforcing and is thus discontinued—the subject ceases to be afraid.

Desensitization

Another important class of procedures included within reciprocal inhibition is referred to as *desensitization* (Paul, 1966; Wolpe, 1958). It too makes use of relaxation and sometimes hypnosis to counteract unrealistic anxiety reactions. In desensitization, Prebyn is hypnotized or trained to relax completely and then asked to imagine some item low on a list of items that are anxiety inducing. Relaxation inhibits the weak level of anxiety that would normally result and Prebyn begins to respond without fear to that item. During the next step of the procedure, Prebyn moves to the second item on the list that elicits a bit more fear or anxiety. Once again the fear response is inhibited. Prebyn gradually proceeds through the list of items that would ordinarily produce more and more anxiety. During later stages Prebyn moves on to confront the real objects associated with the phobia.

Let's say that a cat phobic lists touching and handling cats as the most distressing, seeing a cat through a window (across the street or in a cage) as an intermediate fear, and seeing pictures of cats as distasteful but not actually frightening. We would begin desensitization by encouraging the phobic to relax and think about cats, then progress to looking at pictures of them, reading about them, and so on. Next the phobic could spend some time watching cats in enclosed areas and not within reach. During the final stages the client could be induced to watch others play with a cat

in the same room, and finally begin to approach and actually handle a cat. Throughout the process there is a gradual
buildup of parts in the total experience associated with the
phobic object. At every stage of practice the emphasis is on
relaxation and minimization of anxiety. In fact, if at any
stage the individual experiences anxiety or fear, it is an
indication that the process is progressing too rapidly and
the steps are discontinued, in which case one would return
to a lower step and devise intermediate steps.

Let us take another example, the case of a man who
complains that he cannot drive on freeways. We first ask
him to tell us everything about driving on freeways that he
finds fearful, and then have him rank all of these relative to
one another, from the most to the least distressing. His
fears could include other people driving too close, missing
the appropriate exit ramp, being cut off suddenly by another car, having the car in front stop suddenly, having a
blowout at high speeds, running out of gas with no place
to stop, being involved in a chain-reaction accident, or
skidding on wet pavement during rain.

Each item on such a list is a stimulus that elicits fear
and anxiety, although they may differ in the extent to which
they do so. To help this man produce a novel response to
each of these items, situations are needed in which it is very
difficult for fear to occur in response to any item. First he
must relax completely. Then he is asked to imagine the
least distressing item. Being relaxed inhibits anxiety, and
therefore it is possible to learn a new response to that item.
If the man is able to relax successfully without any sign of
distress in response to this first item, we move up the scale
to the next one, something about freeways that frightens
him slightly more than did the first item. If this in turn is
successful, we try the third item, and so on. This procedure
may take one or two months, since the steps are graded
very finely from least to most feared items, and success is

achieved at each step before progressing. If, as does occasionally happen, the patient becomes quite anxious in response to any one of these situations, it means, as we mentioned above, that we have not graded the situations finely enough. It will then be necessary to find some intermediate situation—between the one that aroused the fear and the last one that was mastered successfully.

Audiovisual aids, such as movies and sound effects that increasingly simulate the feared situation, can also be helpful. The freeway phobic might, at some stage during his desensitization, be shown freeway driving in movies that simulate the view of the driver (as in drivers' training films). This technique might be especially good if he is terrified of rapidly moving vehicles.

Additional steps might involve having the man actually confront the freeway situation in a relaxed state. A situation could be devised in which the chances of risk are minimal and the actual confrontation is also minimal. Accompanied by a good driver whom he trusts, the patient might merely drive from one entrance ramp to the next exit ramp, very early in the morning or late at night when there is little traffic. This design provides the reassurance of a competent companion and maximally safe driving conditions. If the patient can accomplish this feat, he can drive again under similar circumstances but for a longer distance, then with more and more traffic, and so forth.

As the phobic attempts each of these steps, a new reaction is being learned to the act of driving on the freeway. He is learning to be relaxed, not afraid. Although the conditions under which he begins are safe compared to rush-hour traffic, the fact of stimulus generalization remains, so that we can expect him to be able to relax more and more in freeway conditions that involve increasing degrees of danger, provided we continue to move him slowly from step to step.

Rehearsal

Some of the techniques already discussed suggest that learning the skills for dealing with a critical situation can be facilitated by practice under similar circumstances that do not evoke as much negative feeling as the critical situation. There is a wealth of experimental evidence on this subject, and it suggests that learning transfers most readily to those tasks that most resemble the original learning task. This general finding is practiced quite intuitively and is by no means an extraordinary conclusion—its implications appear in our culture in various rules of thumb. Training situations for dangerous types of work or sports (parachuting, ski jumping, air emergency procedures for a stewardess), are devised in such a way that they are analogous to the actual one, but exclude most of the dangerous elements. Military maneuvers, as part of the preparation for the battlefield, illustrate the extreme to which people simulate real and critical situations. Dress rehearsals for plays or concerts are held for essentially the same reason. Some individuals might even rehearse an important job interview with a friend prior to the encounter.

Let us briefly consider the process of rehearsal in terms of conditioning. In essence, it is the learning of responses to noncritical stimuli that gradually resemble the critical stimuli that elicit strong negative emotional reactions. Fear reactions interfere with learning because they cause certain responses that inhibit correct performance and minimize the occurrence of novel responses in the situation. Minimizing fear increases the possibility that new responses can be learned in the situation. Then the learning can be generalized gradually to other stimuli that resemble the highly emotional one more and more.

Thus, even when a rehearsal situation is relatively artificial, if it resembles in some important respects the more critical and difficult problem, our success might be sufficiently positively reinforcing to encourage us to exert further effort at successive stages. However, we also must remember that since the sense of mastery at each stage is an important positive reinforcer, the successive rehearsal stages should be difficult enough so that a sense of mastery is attained following each stage. This means that too many detailed and very similar rehearsal situations must be avoided. Let us consider an everyday problem where rehearsal can be helpful.

Moot: Many times when I attempt to express myself, I have to stop and form the verbal expression of what I am thinking. This often results in my inability to say anything for several long seconds, which is quite embarrassing.

Rehearsal for Moot would involve situations varying along two dimensions: (1) gradual decrease of planning what he is going to say, and (2) gradual increase of listeners, particularly those who may evaluate him critically. First, while alone, Moot could read a certain amount of text and recite it aloud. This situation would involve no listener and Moot would already have the ideas he wished to express. The next step could involve a similar procedure, but would include a friend (a nonevaluative and nonthreatening person) to listen to his recitation. At subsequent stages he would restrict his speaking at social gatherings to more structured materials such as stories or jokes.

Meanwhile, when by himself he could use a tape recorder to practice talking spontaneously. During the final stages of rehearsal, he might talk spontaneously to close friends in preparation for spontaneous conversations with strangers or evaluative persons.

In citing Moot's example, we had to present the progressive steps arbitrarily. In an actual case of rehearsal, Moot himself would assist by deciding how large a step he felt would be feasible at each point to bring him closer to his goal.

Summary

The first concept introduced in this chapter was that every response is determined by a given stimulus or situation, and that the control of the situation can thus provide control over the behaviors that occur in it. A second aspect of stimulus-response relationships is that the presentation of a stimulus that at first does not elicit a response, followed regularly by an unconditioned stimulus that does produce that response, eventually causes the first stimulus alone to elicit the response. This basic idea of conditioning explains a large number of emotional reactions and constitutes a basis for reciprocal inhibition.

Reciprocal inhibition is a powerful technique that is applied to overcome anxiety that has been inadvertently conditioned to certain stimuli, such as phobic reactions (fear of heights, animals, or certain activities). In applying the method, Prebyn is induced to engage in some activity, such as eating or relaxation, which counteracts his or her anxiety reaction at the physiological level. While doing so, Prebyn faces the feared object—or, at first, some object that resembles the feared one, gradually increasing exposure to the feared object until he or she can face it without fear.

The related technique, rehearsal, is based on the premise that it is easier to transfer knowledge or skills from one area to another similar area than to a dissimilar one. Therefore, solution of a problem is best achieved by starting with a similar, but easier, task and then proceeding to more difficult steps gradually. By learning to function successfully during the easier stages of rehearsal, one can be confident and relaxed since the threat of failure or danger is minimal. This relaxation generalizes to the next, more difficult step, making it in turn easier to overcome and so on until one finally learns to function with relative ease in a situation that originally provoked anxiety.

In closing we need to briefly compare the four techniques of reciprocal inhibition, desensitization, forced exposure, and rehearsal to consider the conditions under which each might be most appropriate. Rehearsal is readily distinguished from the others because it is used to counteract realistic fears or dangers, whereas the other three are used with more unrealistic fears or anxieties.

Among the other three, forced exposure or implosive therapy would seem to require a very trusting relationship between Prebyn and Ragent. It can best be used when fear is moderate, with reciprocal inhibition and particularly desensitization being used for the extremes.

Desensitization is a special case of reciprocal inhibition that relies on relaxation to counteract anxiety. The other means of inhibition discussed—eating, strenuous physical activity, or self-assertion—have more limited application and can be used only in special circumstances. For instance, it would be somewhat impractical to use eating to inhibit one person's fears in a vast number of situations. Thus, another rule of thumb could be to use desensitization techniques, rather than some of the other inhibitors, for severe and more pervasive problems (Wolpe, 1969). So, when a person expresses difficulties or is anxious in relationships with relatives, friends, and at work, desensitization might be the appropriate technique. If, in contrast, the person simply has a fear of heights or some specific class of objects, some of the other inhibitors may be easier to use and provide a quick resolution to the problem.

Finally, for less severe problems, reciprocal inhibition can be readily used by psychologically untrained persons, whereas desensitization is more elaborate and time consuming and requires greater familiarity with relaxation techniques. Thus, a mother whose child is afraid of the dark might herself think of a way to counteract the child's fear, but she might have more difficulty applying desensitization if the child refused ever to be left alone.

Some problems are difficult because they contain many parts that differ in level of severity. This final chapter outlines a method of organized approach to difficult problems and involves (1) the identification of component problems, (2) their ordering in terms of levels of severity, and (3) solution of component problems starting with the easiest and progressing to the most difficult.

Chapter 4

PLAN OF APPROACH TO MULTIPROBLEM SITUATIONS

TRANSITIONS FROM EASY TO DIFFICULT

In this final chapter we need to elaborate on the principle of beginning with the behavior that is easiest to change and gradually proceeding to the more difficult. This is particularly important when complex problems are involved, in which several behaviors require change. Indeed, even when only one behavior needs to be changed, special analogues of it may be devised that are simpler and serve as practice for the more difficult aspects of the change that is required.

In general, whenever we are trying to learn something that is novel and difficult, we may anticipate possible failure —no gain for our efforts, pain, and loss of face or self-respect. Furthermore, if we have failed before when attempting to learn this new behavior, trying it again may be associated with vague (or not so vague) feelings of distress and anxiety. Learning proceeds more slowly when there is a high degree of anxiety, so that the presence of strong negative feelings can be distracting and can diminish the possibility of success in changing behavior patterns. It follows that in learning new social skills, or attempting changes in others' behaviors, we would find it helpful to order hierarchically the various aspects of the required change. The changes listed at the bottom of the hierarchy would not only be easier (i.e., associated with less negative feelings due to anticipated failure) but would also, once accomplished, provide us with skills we did not previously possess. The latter in turn would ease the difficulty of mastering the progressively higher steps in the hierarchy.

A third reason to order changes in this way, again, is that when a person succeeds (when we are positively reinforced for our efforts) at one part of a task, we are more likely to continue and persist in trying another part. Starting with the easy parts of a problem helps to insure that our anticipation of positive reinforcement will exceed our expectation of negative reinforcement.

The whole idea of progressing from easier to more difficult steps may be summed up nicely with an African proverb: "The best way to eat the elephant standing in your path is to cut him up in little pieces."

COMPLEX PROBLEMS

In tackling the simple, limited interpersonal problems we all face from day to day we will probably find that one or the other of the techniques described in this monograph would probably serve effectively in each case. Very frequently even those who seek professional help can be assisted sufficiently with only a single technique. But sooner or later most of us encounter difficulties of greater complexity, more pervasive problems that we can't seem to cope with on such simple bases. One example of such a pervasive problem is the experience of a general malaise or discomfort without even knowing why.

There are several general guidelines for an approach to such complex situations, most of which have already been discussed in other contexts. The first step, of course, is to define the problem in terms of its various behavior components. Such a definition provides the details about (1) the kinds of social situations involved; (2) the specific behaviors of the participants as identified through recurrent patterns in the various examples; (3) the duration of the problem, which reveals the rigidity of the behaviors involved; (4) the inadequacy associated with various component behaviors; (5) the reinforcers that may be maintaining each problem behavior; and (6) other reinforcers that can be used to change it. In other words, with our greater familiarity with reinforcement and conditioning techniques, we can now more readily pinpoint the relevant recurrent patterns in a problem situation. As we listen to someone describe various instances in which he or she encounters difficulty, we will be looking for the common patterns noted above.

Another important guideline for dealing with complex problems is that the positively reinforcing results of a change must exceed its negatively reinforcing consequences. Furthermore, any changed behavior that becomes strongly positively reinforcing will be maintained longer than one that is less positively or even negatively reinforcing. Finally, the more rigid and long established a behavior, the more difficult it is to change, since successful change first requires an initial disorganization of the rigid behaviors and then their replacement with other, more reinforcing ones.

Let us briefly consider how these guidelines can be applied in therapy situations.

The therapist would first obtain a definition of the problem and then order the components using some of the procedures from desensitization or rehearsal. George Kelly's (1955) approach, for one, used rehearsal in tackling graded series of problems. He would sometimes write a character sketch that illustrated the patient's mode of behaving in a given situation but differed in some significant respects. He would request the patient to act out this character sketch in a number of situations that increasingly approximated the critical one, or he would modify the sketch to include greater and more difficult changes.

Various stages might involve the use of models for situations where the patient lacks coping skills and feels completely helpless. The therapist could either suggest the models or select one or two from those described as available by the patient. The therapist would use his or her greater awareness of principles of change and of possible roles appropriate to a given situation and suggest several of these to the patient, who in turn would select one or more that feel most comfortable to try. When the patient tried these roles, he or she would first be expected to rehearse them in emotionally neutral situations and then gradually move on to try them in more emotionally arousing (real life) situations.

In the case of married couples, once again the therapist would obtain a detailed list of troublesome incidents with several illustrations of each, in order to define their difficulties vis-à-vis one another. The therapist would also ask them to rate the problems in terms of difficulty. They could next consider how, in the case of the simplest problem, each party could alter his or her behavior to provide a greater degree of positive reinforcement to the other.

These alternate behaviors could be identified by asking each partner to suggest ways in which one would prefer the other to behave. The more acceptable one of these ways would then be attempted. In this way, with some effort, each would gain a desired change in the partner. The therapist's role would therefore consist of helping to identify compromise possibilities and clearly defining such compromises for each party.

The couple would then use appropriate techniques to try one set of changes for about a week. They would return and discuss these changes, modifying the ones that prove unworkable, or simply proceeding with a more difficult step. The therapy situation would thus become an arena for discussing the details of compromise that would gradually be carried over to everyday situations. Having discovered the techniques whereby workable changes in the behaviors of both partners could be defined and attempted, the couple would begin to rely less and less on the therapist.

As in the case of individual therapy, the negative effects of the effort required from each partner would be compensated by the positive gains obtained from changes in the other's behavior. One of the therapist's major contributions would be assistance in identifying alternate behaviors that would maximize reward for both parties and in this way maintain their motivation at various stages.

It is seen then that behavior therapy is more a learning situation than a conventional therapist-patient relationship. Another of its novelties is that it allows the therapist to assume the role of consultant to parents, teachers, or nurses who, in relation to the children and patients involved, would do the bulk of the therapeutic work themselves.

In closing, we should reconsider the one most important way in which our approach differs from psychodynamic and common-sense views of social influence. Both psychodynamic and common-sense notions would suggest that change starts from within (attitudes, feelings, and beliefs) and proceeds outward (specific behaviors). One must change a feeling or belief in order to bring about any lasting change in behavior.

The present approach to social influence would emphasize more the opposite: if behaviors can be changed, and if those changes can be successfully maintained over a period of time, then attitudes, beliefs, and feelings will also change to become consistent with these new behaviors. Accordingly, we end with E. Robert Jones' more eloquent statement:

"It is easier to act yourself into a new way of thinking than to think yourself into a new way of acting."

REFERENCES

Ayllon, T., & Azrin, N. H. *The token economy: A motivational system for therapy and rehabilitation.* New York: Appleton-Century-Crofts, 1968.

Azrin, N. H., & Holz, W. C. Punishment. In W. K. Honig (Ed.), *Operant behavior: Areas of research and application.* New York: Appleton-Century-Crofts, 1966.

Bachrach, A. J. (Ed.) *Experimental foundations of clinical psychology.* New York: Basic Books, 1962.

Bandura, A. Behavior modification through modeling procedures. In L. Krasner & L. P. Ullmann (Eds.), *Research in behavior modification.* New York: Holt, Rinehart and Winston, 1965.

Bandura, A. *Principles of behavior modification.* New York: Holt, Rinehart and Winston, 1969.

Bandura, A., Grusec, J. E., & Menlove, F. L. Vicarious extinction of avoidance behavior. *Journal of Personality and Social Psychology,* 1967, **5,** 16–23.

Bandura, A., & Walters, R. M. *Social learning and personality development.* New York: Holt, Rinehart and Winston, 1963.

Beakel, N. G., & Mehrabian, A. Inconsistent communications and psychopathology. *Journal of Abnormal Psychology,* 1969, **74,** 126–130.

Bijou, S. W., & Baer, D. M. Operant methods in child behavior and development. In W. K. Honig (Ed.), *Operant behavior: Areas of research and application.* New York: Appleton-Century-Crofts, 1966.

Brady, J. V. Operant methodology and the experimental production of altered physiological states. In W. K. Honig (Ed.), *Operant behavior: Areas of research and application*. New York: Appleton-Century-Crofts, 1966.

Buehler, R. E., Patterson, G. R., & Furniss, J. M. The reinforcement of behaviour in institutional settings. *Behavior Research and Therapy*, 1966, **4**, 157–167.

Engel, B. T., & Hansen, S. P. Operant conditioning of heart rate speeding. *Psychophysiology*, 1967, **3**, 418–426.

Erikson, E. H. *Childhood and society*. New York: W. W. Norton, 1963.

Eysenck, H. J. (Ed.) *Behavior therapy and the neuroses*. New York: Macmillan, 1960.

Ferster, C. B., & Skinner, B. F. *Schedules of reinforcement*. New York: Appleton-Century-Crofts, 1957.

Freud, S. *A general introduction to psychoanalysis*. New York: Doubleday, 1935.

Guthrie, E. R. *The psychology of learning*. New York: Harper & Row, 1935.

Heckhausen, H. *The anatomy of achievement motivation*. New York: Academic Press, 1967.

Hefferline, R. F., Keenan, B., & Harford, R. A. Escape and avoidance conditioning in human subjects without their observation of the response. *Science*, 1959, **130**, 1338–1339.

Holt, R. R. Forcible indoctrination and personality change. In P. Worchel & D. Byrne (Eds.), *Personality change*. New York: Wiley, 1964.

Jacobson, E. *Progressive relaxation*. Chicago: University of Chicago Press, 1938.

Kelly, G. *The psychology of personal constructs*. New York: W. W. Norton, 1955.

Keutzer, C. S. Behavior modification of smoking: A review, analysis and experimental application with focus on subject variables as predictors of treatment outcome. Unpublished doctoral dissertation, University of Oregon, 1967.

Keutzer, C. S., Lichtenstein, E., & Mees, H. L. Modification of smoking behavior: A review. *Psychological Bulletin*, 1968, **70**, 520–533.

Lovaas, O. I., Schaffer, B., & Simmons, J. Q. Building social behavior in autistic children by use of electric shock. *Journal of Experimental Research in Personality*, 1965, **1**, 99–109.

Lundin, R. W. *Personality: A behavioral analysis*. London: Collier-MacMillan, 1969.

McClelland, D. C. *The achieving society*. Princeton, N. J.: D. Van Nostrand, 1961.

Mehrabian, A. *Tactics of social influence.* Englewood Cliffs, N. J.: Prentice-Hall, 1970.

Mehrabian, A. *Silent messages.* Belmont, Calif.: Wadsworth, 1971.

Mehrabian, A. *Nonverbal communication.* Chicago: Aldine-Atherton, 1972.

Mehrabian, A., & Ksionzky, S. *A theory of affiliation.* Lexington, Mass.: D. C. Heath, 1974.

Mehrabian, A., & Reed, H. Factors influencing judgments of psychopathology. *Psychological Reports,* 1969, **24,** 323–330.

Mischel, W. *Personality and assessment.* New York: Wiley, 1968.

Morse, W. H. Intermittent reinforcement. In W. K. Honig (Ed.), *Operant behavior: Areas of research and application.* New York: Appleton-Century-Crofts, 1966.

Paul, G. L. *Insight vs. desensitization in psychotherapy.* Stanford, Calif.: Stanford University Press, 1966.

Premack, D. Reinforcement theory. In D. Levine (Ed.), *Nebraska Symposium on Motivation.* Lincoln: University of Nebraska, 1965.

Rapaport, D. The structure of psychoanalytic theory: A systematizing attempt. In S. Koch (Ed.), *Psychology: A study of a science.* Vol. 3. New York: McGraw-Hill, 1959.

Rogers, C. R. *Client-centered therapy.* Boston: Houghton Mifflin, 1951.

Rosen, J. N. *Direct analysis.* New York: Grune & Stratton, 1953.

Skinner, B. F. *Cumulative record.* (Enlarged ed.) New York: Appleton-Century-Crofts, 1961.

Stampfl, T. G., & Levis, D. J. Essentials of implosive therapy: A learning-theory-based psychodynamic behavioral therapy. *Journal of Abnormal Psychology,* 1967, **72,** 496–503.

Terrace, H. S. Stimulus control. In W. K. Honig (Ed.), *Operant behavior: Areas of research and application.* New York: Appleton-Century-Crofts, 1966.

Tyler, V. O., Jr. Exploring the use of operant techniques in the rehabilitation of deliquent boys. Paper read at American Psychological Association, Chicago, September 1965.

Ullmann, L. P., & Krasner, L. *A psychological approach to abnormal behavior.* Englewood Cliffs, N. J.: Prentice-Hall, 1969.

Watson, J. B., & Rayner, R. Conditioned emotional reactions. *Journal of Experimental Psychology,* 1920, **3,** 1–14.

Williams, C. D. The elimination of tantrum behavior by extinction procedures. *Journal of Abnormal and Social Psychology,* 1959, **59,** 269.

Wolpe, J. *Psychotherapy by reciprocal inhibition.* Stanford, Calif.: Stanford University Press, 1958.

Wolpe, J. *The practice of behavior therapy.* Elmsford, N. Y.: Pergamon Press, 1969.